Sparking the Thinking of Students,
Ages 10-14

Strategies for Teachers

Glenda Ward Beamon

CORWIN PRESS, INC.
A Sage Publications Company
Thousand Oaks, California

For information:

Corwin Press, Inc.
A Sage Publications Company
2455 Teller Road
Thousand Oaks, California 91320
E-mail: order@corwin.sagepub.com

SAGE Publications Ltd.
6 Bonhill Street
London EC2A 4PU
United Kingdom

SAGE Publications India Pvt. Ltd.
M-32 Market
Greater Kailash I
New Delhi 110 048 India

Library of Congress Cataloging-in-Publication Data

Beamon, Glenda Ward.
    Sparking the thinking of students, ages 10-14: strategies
for teachers / by Glenda Ward Beamon.
        p. cm.
    Includes bibliographical references and index.
    ISBN 0-8039-6583-4 (pbk.). — ISBN 0-8039-6582-6 (cloth)
    1. Thought and thinking—Study and teaching (Elementary)
    2. Thought and thinking—Study and teaching (Secondary)
    3. Learning. I. Title.
    LB1590.3.B39 1997
    372.24'2—dc21   97-4796

This book is printed on acid-free paper.

97 98 99 00 01 02 03 10 9 8 7 6 5 4 3 2 1

Production Editor:	Sherrise M. Purdum
Production Assistant:	Denise Santoyo
Editorial Assistant:	Kristen L. Gibson
Typesetter/Designer:	Danielle Dillahunt
Indexer:	Teri Greenberg
Cover Designer:	Marcia R. Finlayson
Print Buyer:	Anna Chin

Contents

Foreword   vii
David H. Reilly

Preface   xii
  Acknowledgments   xiv

About the Author   xvi

Introduction and Overview   1

1. **Understanding the Changing Times**   5
   Overview   5
   What We Know Now About
     Student Thinking and Learning   7
   The Developmental Nature
     of the Young Adolescent Learner   9
   Making Classrooms "Safe"
     for Young Adolescent Thinking   12
   Summary   15

2. **Creating a Safe for Thinking Climate**   17
   Overview   17
   Raise Expectations and Extend Opportunities   18

When Thinking Is Most Likely to Happen 20
Attitudes—Theirs and Yours 22
How Challenge Can Motivate 23
What Does Thinking Look Like? 24
Adding Enough Rigor to Collaborative Learning 26
The "Safe" Middle-Level Classroom 29
Summary 31

3. **Challenging Student Thinking and Learning** 32
   Overview 32
   The "Inside" Story on Students' Brains 33
   How Young Adolescents Learn 35
   The Thinking-Learning Connection 37
   The New View of Intelligence 39
   Cognitive Development and
       the Young Adolescent 42
   The "Thinking-Responsive"
       Middle-Level Classroom 44
   Summary 46

4. **Interacting Through Questioning and Inquiry** 48
   Overview 49
   The Power of Teacher Questioning 49
   Getting All Students to Answer 51
   How to Construct "Safe" Questions 54
   Why the Next Question Matters 59
   Linking Student Thinking With Student Learning 68
   Seminars in Session 71
   TOP TEN List on "How to Fail at Leading
       a Stimulating Discussion" 72
   Inquiry and Interaction
       in the Middle-Level Classroom 73
   Summary 77

5. **Assessing Through Products and Performance** 79
   Overview 79
   What's New in Assessment for
       Young Adolescents and Why 81
   A Few More Examples 86
   The Assessment Dilemma 87
   Performance Assessment and Evaluation 91
   Developmental Assessment in "Process" 94
   When Thinking Is Observable 95
   How to "Rate" Students' Oral Responses 100

How Can We Hold Students
   Accountable for Learning?   104
Meaningful Assessment in
   the Middle-Level Classroom   105
Summary   106

6. **Extending for**
   Meaning and Enrichment   **108**
   Overview   108
   Linking Content With Thinking Processes   109
   Curricular Themes and Real-World Connections   112
   Thematic Planning and
      Young Adolescent Learning   114
   Where Does Performance Fit In?   117
   Dealing With All
      Those Interests and Abilities   121
   Young Adolescent Writers at Work   124
   How Technology Can Be
      a "Turn-On" to Learning   127
   Beyond the Middle-Level Classroom   130
   Summary   132

7. **Anticipating the Challenge Ahead**   **134**
   Overview   134
   Education at the Crossroads   135
   Moving in the Right Direction   137
   The Dynamics of the
      Future Middle-Level Classroom   139
   Summary   145

References   **147**

Index   **153**

To my sons, Michael and Brent,
who have always believed in me.

And to Mike,
who helped me to believe in myself.

Foreword

As anyone interested in the field of education is aware, schooling and student learning outcomes have been the subject of much criticism during the past few decades. Although many books and articles have been written on how to improve this situation, rarely does a book come along that is a carefully blended balance of theory and practical advice crafted into a well designed and sequenced series of ideas for improving learning and thinking skills of students. Dr. Beamon has accomplished this task in *Sparking the Thinking of Students, Ages 10-14*. Her goal was to provide "teachers of young adolescents a current, philosophical, theoretical and practical program to help these students develop and refine thinking abilities." She succeeded admirably.

This book is for teachers who wish to improve their students' thinking skills. The book begins with how to establish a "Safe for Thinking" climate and discusses how this climate is appropriate for meeting developmental needs of young adolescents. Chapter 3 provides an overview of recent developments and new understandings arising from research in cognitive science and how these findings relate to the learning and other needs of young adolescents. Chapter

4 focuses on teacher questioning strategies and the linking of content with student thinking and learning improvement. Chapter 5 deals with assessment. Chapters 6 and 7 are exciting chapters. Chapter 6 addresses how teachers can make their classrooms a connection between the curriculum and the real world. Chapter 7 looks ahead to classrooms for young adolescents that can challenge and excite them by capitalizing on their interests. Liberal use of actual classroom activities and scenarios in each chapter provide the reader many examples and illustrations that can be used in his/her own class.

One of the key aspects of this book is the Safe for Thinking program Dr. Beamon developed to improve and expand thinking skills in young adolescents. It is based on the assumption that young adolescent learning and thinking are interactive, progressive, and developmental processes. This program draws on our knowledge of adolescent development and recent findings from the expanding research base of cognitive science. The findings from these two areas of research are integrated with Dr. Beamon's extensive experience as a teacher of middle-grade students to produce a progressive sequence of steps to aid young adolescents think more effectively.

Dr. Beamon has been both a gifted classroom teacher and researcher on how young adolescents learn, develop, and think. The combination of these experiences is evident in her approach to this book. She draws on extensive experience as a former middle-grades teacher and the examples and classroom scenarios she portrays are authentic. These examples and scenarios are carefully used to illustrate how the developmental, and particularly the thinking, needs of young adolescents can be nurtured within a Safe for Thinking classroom. The role of the teacher as guide for improving the thinking skills of students is highlighted throughout the book.

Dr. Beamon has developed the concept of a classroom that is Safe for Thinking for young adolescents in recognition of their developmental status and the tumultuous events that are going on in their lives during these years. In addition to the concept of such a classroom, Dr. Beamon has designed an inquiry program for establishing a classroom climate that is conducive for young adolescents to experiment with their thinking skills. Students also learn to expand these skills within an environment that is safe for such efforts, and indeed, expects and encourages such experimentation.

The key figure in establishing this type of classroom is the teacher. As Dr. Beamon makes clear early in the book, it is one written for teachers of, "energy and enthusiasm, of action and interaction, of creativity and purpose." It is also written for the "educator who values and accepts the ideas of youth." Clearly, Dr. Beamon is an educator who values children and this credo comes across strongly throughout the book; so also does her energy and enthusiasm for the classroom. This is not a book of easily followed recipes. Implementing Dr. Beamon's program will require teachers who are thinkers themselves, who can think on their feet, and most of all, teachers who know their students' developmental status and needs. Teachers who follow the suggestions of how to improve young adolescents' thinking skills will find that it requires dedication, hard effort, and continuous attentiveness to students' individual and group needs and developmental status during class activities and discussions.

Dr. Beamon has used her classroom experiences to embed the Safe for Thinking program into a carefully researched and articulated knowledge base of the developmental status and needs of young adolescents. Within this base of young adolescent development she has meticulously addressed the cognitive and thinking skill need of this age group. Drawing on the work of Leslie Hart and Howard Gardner, among others, she has designed her strategies for teachers, a taxonomy that assists students in a sequenced progression to learn to think better and to learn to evaluate their own thinking skill level.

It is this careful integration of practical experience, knowledge of young adolescent development, and knowledge of what this age group needs in order to learn and think better that forms the core of this book. The classroom climate that can be generated by following the Safe for Thinking program leads to students feeling safe and secure in trying a variety of cognitive approaches in learning to more effectively problem solve as well as learning to generalize to real-life situations. It is the feeling of acceptance in the classroom as well as the expectation and encouragement for achieving higher levels of thinking that characterizes the Safe for Thinking class. Teachers that follow this approach act as guides and facilitators for improving students' thinking skills.

The Safe for Thinking program is designed to aid students improve their thinking processes, to learn to evaluate their own thinking skills, and to progress in their ability to problem solve and generalize. It is concerned equally with content, process, progress, and product. The need for clearly communicated criteria for quality standards for thinking and learning is emphasized so that students know where they stand in relation to the teacher's expectations. As important, they learn what they must do to advance in their thinking skill development.

Assessment of students' thinking processes and progress is a major consideration in this book. Dr. Beamon devotes an entire chapter ("Assessing Through Products and Performance") to this topic. Two critical issues are addressed. The first is how to assess students' thinking skill development. Assessing students' thinking requires a more sophisticated approach than simply asking them to respond to a multiple choice exam or to a series of essay questions. It requires ongoing assessment that must be carefully linked to planning the goals of the lesson and the appropriate classroom procedures. This chapter details several procedures that teachers can use to conduct ongoing assessment of students' progress in learning to think more effectively.

The second issue addressed in this chapter is the difference between norm referenced testing and assessment of thinking development. This is a most important issue. Given the national investment in the use of norm referenced tests and states' requirements for such tests, the use of process assessment is bound to raise controversy. Dr. Beamon makes a strong case for the use of process assessment and provides convincing arguments for parents, educators, and others to adopt process assessment as the best means of helping students' thinking skills improve.

This is a good book. Its significance lies in providing an optimistic view of what can be done to aid students to think more effectively. It is optimistic about what can be done to excite, challenge, and reward young adolescents who are striving to understand themselves and the world around them. We have too few books that offer an optimistic view of students and schooling. This is one that does.

The book is also significant because it speaks from teacher to teacher. It is founded in actual classroom experiences, aided and refined by an understanding of what young adolescents want and need, and by using cognitive research to hone the strategies that will elicit their best thinking.

Teacher education students would do will to emulate the enthusiasm for teaching that is portrayed. Older, more experienced teachers will find new and meaningful ways to help their students think better, learn more effectively, and be able to apply what they have learned to real world situations. School administrators will find this book helpful in assisting teachers teach their students to think and learn more effectively and curriculum supervisors will find it of immense help.

David H. Reilly, Ed.D., ABPP, FAASP
Dean, College of Graduate and Professional Studies
The Citadel
Charleston, SC

Preface

Early adolescence, spanning the years from 10 to 14 years of age, is a time of vulnerability and awakening. It is a formative period when physical change accelerates, social exploration is tentative, and mental capacity is rapidly unfolding. It is a time of opportunity for middle-school teachers—a time to capitalize on intellectual potential and positively affect student cognitive development. This book offers middle-level teachers a realistic and manageable instructional approach that is based on an understanding of how young adolescents think, learn, and develop intellectually.

It has been my experience as a teacher of young adolescents, as a doctoral student in the area of preadolescent cognitive development, and as a supervisor of student teachers in Grades 5 through 9, to look in many classrooms. Often I observed teacher-student interaction practices that minimized students' involvement and limited higher-level thinking expression. Teacher questions were posed in a "rapid-fire" fashion with seemingly little thought to cognitive level, sequence, or process. Students were expected to respond just as rapidly, supplying specific answers to the low-level and predictable questions. Most of the interaction was teacher initiated and teacher controlled. Infrequently were students asked to elaborate, support, and explain responses, or pose personal questions.

At other times I observed classrooms in which true inquiry was apparent. The interaction pattern could be described as star shaped, with students responding to teacher-initiated questions, as well as asking and responding to each others' questions. Teacher questioning was purposeful, with thought obviously given to level and follow-up. Probing questions indicated the expectation for students to think more deeply about a response, to substantiate answers, or to try and describe the thinking used to arrive at a particular response. Wait-time following questions and after student responses could actually be counted in seconds. Although fewer questions were asked, richer discussion was obvious, and students were motivated and active participants. The environment was "safe" for thinking, standards were high, and quality thinking was evident.

Observations in yet other middle-level classrooms indicated purposeful instruction intended to challenge young adolescent thinking; these practices, however, often failed to accomplish the teacher's goal. Learning groups in which students worked together on tasks, for example, encouraged student interaction and discussion, yet they lacked the sufficient structure, challenge, or relevancy of purpose needed to motivate and hold the attention of young adolescent learners. Roles were not assigned, expected behaviors were not communicated, and criteria for evaluation were often unclear to students. Other teachers involved students in investigative research projects, scientific experiments, problem solving, and debates, yet failed to maximize these group learning experiences with purposefully structured tasks, an expectation for accountability, and specific standards for quality of work.

My intention in the preceding scenarios is not to imply a lack of interest among current middle-level teachers in helping young adolescents become better thinkers. On the contrary, I would venture that few teachers at this level cling to the conventional belief that cognitive development is "on hold" during the early adolescent years. Most teachers in my experiences are genuinely interested in helping young adolescents develop thinking abilities. What seems to be lacking, however, is a framework that would help teachers better connect the teaching of thinking with the developmental needs of the young adolescent learner.

The Safe for Thinking approach described in this book is intended to give teachers of young adolescents a current, philosophical, theoretical, and practical program to help these students develop and refine thinking abilities. This approach combines current and emerging cognitive theory about how the mind operates with developmentally appropriate middle-level instruction. Characterized by a supportive, expectant, and challenging learning environment, observable student involvement, responsibility, accountability, relevant subject matter, and meaningful assessment, this framework can be applied across any discipline and curriculum through the flexible and strategic decision making of the middle-level teacher.

This book is written for the educator of energy and enthusiasm, of action and interaction, of creativity and purpose. It is written for the educator who values and accepts the ideas of youth, and who is not satisfied until the ideas mature into more thoughtful expression. It is written for the educator who is versatile and flexible, seemingly risking "control" for the sake of more student-initiated thinking and learning. It is also written for the teacher who realizes that to encourage and expect students to question and wonder, to suppose and hypothesize, and to consider novel possibilities is to nurture the thinking leadership of the next generation.

Acknowledgments

This book celebrates the spirit of those who helped to make it happen. To these special individuals, I offer the following heartfelt appreciation.

To my seventh-grade teacher, Nancy Howell Toney, who taught me the value of intellectual challenge. This book is a tribute to her impact on the lives of countless young adolescents in the Burlington City Schools.

To the exemplary teachers who inspired the various scenarios—I celebrate their belief in the capacity of the young adolescent mind, and I hope I adequately captured the dynamics of their Safe for Thinking classrooms.

To my former young adolescent students—I rejoice in their creative energy and a "million unanswered questions." Their voices can be heard from each page.

To my parents, Claude and Polly Ward, who faithfully took care of me and my summer roses. As usual, their help was unquestioningly given.

To my friend Heather, whose assistance ranged from scribbled notes of reassurance to late-night editing. Her sweet spirit carried me.

To my sons, Michael and Brent, for their patience, their sense of humor, and their unwavering source of pride. They are my best cheerleaders, my strongest allies, and my closest friends.

To David H. Reilly, my mentor, colleague, and friend. He encouraged me to write what I believe, and he believed that I could do it well. Through his support and assistance, my fondest dream has come true.

About the Author

Glenda Ward Beamon's experience with the young adolescent learner spans a period of 20 years. She has taught Grades 4 through 11, and currently coordinates the middle-school program at Elon College in North Carolina, where she also chairs the Department of Teacher Education, teaches, and directs the Master of Education program. A recipient of system and state-level outstanding teaching awards, she is active as a consultant in the areas of critical thinking, multiple intelligences, gifted education, and inquiry-based questioning. She presents regularly at state, national, and international conferences, and has published articles on the Safe for Thinking classroom. She was an exchange professor at Southeast University in Nanjing, Peoples' Republic of China, and with the University of London in England. Avid travelers, she and her sons, Michael and Brent, reside in Burlington.

Introduction
and Overview

This book is written for teachers who want to create a learning environment that supports and challenges young adolescent thinking. In this setting, the many dimensions of classroom life function in harmony to create a synergy of interaction. These dynamics are visible among students in their exchange of ideas, in the inquisitive energy of their questioning, in the developing intellectual depth of their verbal and written expression, and in their growing sense of responsibility, leadership, and personal accountability. It is noticeable in the teachers' purposeful and challenging use of questioning strategies, in students' opportunity to interact meaningfully in large and small groups, and in the teachers' treatment of students' thinking and learning efforts.

It is noticeable in the teachers' creative attempts to individualize and vary students' learning experiences and in the anticipated quality of their learning products. The expectation for students is that they think, respond, substantiate, elaborate, create, and design; the expectation for teachers is that they encourage, accept, guide, facilitate, motivate, and challenge. The climate of this learning environment is purposefully established to help young adolescents feel emotionally and cognitively "safe" to use and extend their developing intellectual capacities.

The Safe for Thinking approach is based on the assumption that young adolescent learning and thinking are interactive, progressive, and developmental processes. It is anticipated that this book will help middle-level educators gain the knowledge and skills needed to create a more intellectually challenging classroom environment. Each chapter presents current research with practical application for the middle-level teacher, and integrates these instructional approaches with the developmental needs of the young adolescent. Chapters 2 through 7 highlight scenarios of middle-level classrooms to illustrate the cognitive theory-into-practice. Varying in discipline and spanning the Grade levels of 5 through 9, these classrooms reflect a Safe for Thinking climate and developmentally appropriate, thinking-responsive instruction. The scenarios are constructed from data collected through actual classroom visits.

Chapter 1 offers a general overview of current cognitive research and its implication for teachers who seek to structure a learning environment conducive to young adolescent thinking development. This chapter highlights the developmental nature of the young adolescent learner who is experiencing an emerging capacity for intellectual development and establishes the need for cognitive-based instruction at this grade level.

Chapter 2 describes the foundational conditions, both affective and cognitive, of a classroom climate "safe" for young adolescent thinking. Teacher and student thinking-supportive attitudes and behaviors are proposed and linked specifically to the developmental needs of the young adolescent student. The eighth-grade math class profiled in Chapter 2 reflects a "safe" learning environment in which students willingly engage in collaborative problem solving.

Chapter 3 focuses on the cognitive development of the young adolescent with application of recent and exciting findings from brain research. It also presents new and expanded views of intelligence and explains the critical learning-thinking connection. The sixth-grade science classroom featured in Chapter 3 models a thinking-responsive student-centered classroom in which choice allows for exploration of multiple intelligences.

Chapter 4 delves into inquiry-based instruction with specific teacher questioning strategies that challenge both the level of student thinking and its depth. A questioning model and techniques for seminar discussion are linked to the social and intellectual development of the young adolescent. The sixth-grade language arts classroom illustrated in Chapter 5 profiles inquiry-based discussion with emphasis on the teacher's use of questioning that stimulates student higher-level thinking processes.

Chapter 5 deals with the challenge of meaningful assessment and addresses the following questions: How does one know when the classroom dynamics indicate a thinking climate? How does one know when students' responses reflect improved reasoning skills, better logic, or more thoughtful expression? How does one motivate students to become evaluators of their own intellectual maturation? How might performance and other learning products be evaluated? The seventh-grade social studies classroom described in Chapter 5 demonstrates teacher-student interaction and illustrates student involvement in product selection and assessment.

Chapter 6 takes a look at other instructional methods for the thinking development of young adolescent students. Thematic and interdisciplinary unit development, writing and reading responses, technology, community action projects, and suggestions for student products and performance are presented in a context of helping the young adolescent make the developmental transition toward responsibility and leadership. The eighth-grade language arts classroom detailed in Chapter 6 models a writing workshop with its emphasis on the progression toward student ownership in the writing process. A collaborative teacher-student project that uses technology to create an awareness of young adolescent literature is also described.

Chapter 7 projects the direction of middle-level education in light of cognitive science and the thrust for more meaningful instruction and learning. A future classroom scenario is projected in anticipation of the challenge that lies ahead for the educator of young adolescent students.

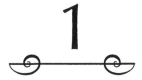

Understanding the Changing Times

Dear, dear! How queer everything is today! And yesterday things went on just as usual. I wonder if I've changed during the night? Let me think: Was I the same when I got up this morning? I almost think I can remember feeling a little different. But if I'm not the same, the next question is "Who in the world am I?" Ah, that's the great puzzle.

Alice

Alice in Wonderland (Lewis Carroll, 1971, pp. 15-16)

Overview

Thirty-five years ago, before such terms as cognitive instruction, integrated curriculum, multiple intelligences, authentic assessment, and "developmentally appropriate" were common vernacular among educators, I was a student in Miss Howell's seventh-grade classroom. My classmates and I were 12-year-olds, precariously traversing that middle ground of young adolescence. We were trying out ideas and trying on identities, moving tentatively within a newly perceived social context while gaining perspective and negotiating confidence. Our minds were beginning to consider abstract notions and to be concerned with such concepts as peace, morality, and justice. It was a time when the United States had as its mission ridding the world of communism, the South was beginning to reconsider lingering racial attitudes, and a visionary young president from New England was inaugurated. It was a time of possibilities for the world and for ourselves, and we were eager to consider them. Miss Howell's classroom provided us that "safe" place.

Miss Howell, with her tolerance for the ambiguity, sense of immortality and self-righteous airs of our pubescent natures, allowed my classmates and me to share thoughts and test emerging personal theories about the world and our place in it. We discussed, debated, wrote, designed, created, presented, performed, and evaluated. We cooked, traveled, conducted experiments and research, and learned foreign languages. We also developed intellectually, socially, and emotionally in this atmosphere of acceptance, interaction, and challenge. Miss Howell's was a classroom that was "safe" for thinking, and she not only permitted it—she encouraged and expected it.

Teachers of young adolescents today live in the best of all possible times. Admittedly, the challenge of motivating this diverse and energetic group of students is no simple matter. Three decades ago, Miss Howell's instructional decisions seemed based on an intuitive understanding of the learning process. She recognized the need for student choice, involvement, and exploration; her questions elevated students' level of thinking; and she understood the value of meaningful assignments, meaningful inquiry, and meaningful evaluation. Miss Howell taught her 12-year-olds in a seemingly timeless fashion, and she did it well.

Much has changed since Miss Howell stood before that particular seventh-grade class. What this master teacher did well then is supported now by a theoretical framework that today's teachers of young adolescents can readily put into classroom practice. New cognitive research has generated a clearer understanding of the internal activity of students' brains as they are involved in thinking and learning. Theories about the classroom conditions that support or inhibit the thinking and learning process have gained acceptance. Middle school philosophy has offered a developmental context through which curriculum and instruction can be made more responsive to the needs of the young adolescent learner. A teacher's ability to make strategic decisions about instructional techniques, grouping, grading, and curriculum development has become a skill of increasing importance.

This chapter presents a brief overview of recent and pertinent cognitive research as it applies to teaching students, ages 10 to 14. It also addresses the developmental nature of young adolescent learners and characterizes a classroom environment "safe" for young adolescent thinking development.

What We Know Now About
Student Thinking and Learning

John Dewey (1933), in his book, *How We Think*, suggested that a student's mind is not a piece of blot paper that absorbs and retains information automatically. He made the following observation:

> It is hardly an exaggeration to say that too often the pupil is treated as if he were a phonographic record on which is impressed a set of words that are to be literally reproduced . . . the mind is treated as it if were a cistern into which information is conducted by one set of pipes that mechanically pour it in. (p. 260)

Dewey's early metaphors about thinking and learning foreshadow the direction of the cognitive research in the latter part of the 20th century. Recent cognitive theory is based on the premise that student thinking and learning are processes that involve a purposeful exchange among students and teachers. Current cognitive development theory, new views about the nature of intelligence, and recent findings from brain research support the notion that thinking and learning take place best in a supportive, interactive, and challenging classroom environment.

New and emerging cognitive theory refers to certain dynamics that are created when teachers establish specific classroom conditions that promote and sustain student thinking and learning. An underlying belief among current theorists is that thinking is a highly complex endeavor, sensitive to factors internal to the student and external in his or her environment (Hart, 1983; Sternberg, 1984). The trend over the past three decades has been to view students' abilities as what they bring to different thinking and learning situations, rather than as fixed indicators of individual capabilities (Bruner, 1964; Clark, 1983). This enlightened viewpoint focuses positively on possibility, potential, and growth. The challenge for teachers becomes that of "unlocking" students' cognitive capacities by providing them an opportunity to interact within a stimulating and responsive classroom setting.

In his recent book, *A Celebration of Neurons*, Sylwester (1995) questioned how a profession charged with "the development of an effective and efficient human brain can continue to remain uninformed about that brain?" (p. 6). Important and fascinating findings in the area of brain research can provide educators of young adolescents with an understanding of how these students' brains operate during learning activity. An interactive "brain-based" learning environment in which teachers and students are engaged in complex interactions activates the brain and is critical to the thinking and learning process (Caine & Caine, 1991; Sylwester, 1995). Conversely, the traditional, more passive and teacher-dominated classroom arrangement does little to stimulate high-level brain functioning of students.

Another interesting phenomenon in regard to how the brain responds and operates is its tendency to disengage or withdraw from higher levels of processing under conditions of stress, embarrassment, and control (Hart, 1983). When students feel threatened or humiliated, emotions arise that may interfere with thinking capacity. By creating a classroom climate in which students feel supported and valued, teachers can avoid the brain reaction called "downshifting." The brain also tends to "downshift" under conditions of low challenge and limited interaction. Students may perceive a task as meaningless busywork, for example, or, if little opportunity is given to verbalize ideas, minds may wander. In addition, to overstimulate or challenge students beyond their current thinking capacity may similarly trigger this thinking-adverse brain reaction. To help students make optimal use of thinking capacity, then, teachers must try to provide an appropriate balance of support, encouragement, stimulation, challenge, and complexity.

One other exciting brain research concept of interest to middle-level educators is that of "brain plasticity" (Caine & Caine, 1991). Organized at birth, the brain is ready to interact with the external world and these ongoing experiences are what shape and develop it. Opportunities that provide a variety of rich emotional, social, and cognitive interactions in a safe and consistent context can literally change the physiological structure of the brain and affect its operation (Clark, 1983). The brain's thinking capacity can actually increase.

A more in-depth discussion of the brain's functioning during the thinking-learning process is provided in Chapter 3.

Current cognitive research has also challenged the traditional view of how students learn, how learning may be represented, and how it may be assessed. Gardner's (1983) theory of multiple intelligences compels teachers of young adolescents to examine any lingering perceptions that students' cognitive abilities are fixed and one dimensional. Intelligence as a pluralistic reality that can be enhanced within the context of meaningful classroom experiences is a powerful educational phenomenon. Teachers can determine and build on young adolescent students' intellectual strengths and encourage less dominant abilities through carefully designed instruction. They can assess these students' strengths and the quality of performance within a "problem-solving" or "product-fashioning" context, and thus help students become aware of and monitor their own thinking and learning development (Lazear, 1994; Wiggins, 1993). Chapter 3 provides further discussion and instructional application of Gardner's multiple intelligence theory.

These contemporary understandings from cognitive research send a strong message for classroom instruction of the young adolescent student. Although less directive, the teacher's role is more strategically powerful as one who structures the learning environment, designs the lessons, challenges for more complex thinking, and collaboratively monitors the progress. Haglund (1981) suggested that students do not resist the process of thinking and learning; rather, the more traditional classroom settings are "antithetical to inquiring minds" (p. 225). Modern cognitive theorists are in consensus about the importance of an interactive, challenging, and dynamic learning environment in which students are involved in complex thinking and meaningful learning. The challenge for teachers of young adolescents is to create a "thinking climate" that represents a balance among classroom conditions that permit, encourage, support, and expect thinking to happen.

The Developmental Nature
of the Young Adolescent Learner

A popular eighth-grade teacher fondly dubbed young adolescents as "hormonally challenged." They have entered a period of physical and intellectual development more dramatic than any since infancy. Cognitive changes have given them the capacity to think abstractly, to consider alternative perspectives, to make and understand the consequence of personal decisions, and to think about their own thinking. These young adolescents need a "safe" place in which to experiment with this budding capacity for reasoning, introspection, and propositional thinking; they also need intentional instruction that will enable and guide the development of thinking abilities.

Young adolescents furthermore need to form positive peer relationships and caring relationships with adults who like and respect them. They are generally unsure of themselves, and although they are extremely energetic and thrive on experimentation, they need clear structure to help them become responsible decision makers. Young adolescents tend to be self-conscious and self-critical, yet they need opportunities to explore creative and diverse talents and to have their accomplishments recognized by those around them. They need to participate in real-life learning situations, to be creative, and to be active. They also need time to reflect on how they think others perceive them and to integrate these impressions into their evolving self-identities. Students in the age group of 10 to 14 tend to display a wide range of individual intellectual development as their minds experience the transition toward more abstract and higher-level thinking. This capacity opens the potential for interactive, engaged thinking, yet its tentative nature evidences the need for guidance in the direction of thinking proficiency (Schurr, 1989). These young adolescents are internally "negotiating" new thinking capacities and they simultaneously need external assistance to develop the mental habits associated with more disciplined thinking. Teachers need to capitalize on the rapid unfolding of young adolescents' intellectual capacity, thus taking advantage of their readiness for problem solving, reasoning, analysis, and conceptualization. In addition, teachers need to help these students improve the quality of their thinking by expecting and encouraging them to express or write clearly and accurately and to reason logically.

The Carnegie Council on Adolescent Development (1989) report, *Turning Points: Preparing American Youth for the 21st Century*, recognized the critical need for teachers to help young adolescents acquire "flexible and inquiring habits of mind . . . to find constructive expression of their inherent curiosity and exploratory energy . . . to challenge the reliability of evidence, or ideas presented . . . see relationships . . .

[and] to construct knowledge" (pp. 12, 43). These youngsters are intensely inquisitive, favor interaction and active learning, exhibit independent thought, and experience the phenomenon of metacognition, yet they are intellectually "at risk" if these needs are not met (Schurr, 1989). Teachers must set the stage for thinking to happen; they also must reinforce thinking development through the selection of teaching methods, curricular materials, learning tasks and opportunities, and assessment.

Teachers of young adolescents play a strategic role in structuring classroom experiences that respond to these students' expanding cognitive potential. Fortunately, middle school philosophy, with its emphasis on small communities of learning, meaningful interaction, interdisciplinary teaming, and block scheduling provides a favorable context for thinking instruction. Students in this developmental period are encouraged to develop a sense of identity within a supportive, sustained context, and they can also find the opportunity, guidance, and expectation to practice and refine growing cognitive abilities (Van Hoose & Strahan, 1989). These students' thinking abilities are enhanced in supportive classrooms in which teachers communicate that their ideas, questions, and concerns are accepted and valued.

Preparing for a "safe" thinking environment requires a teacher and student mind-set that thinking will happen and that it will be respected. Teachers of young adolescents must be willing to cast aside any preconceived ideas about these students' thinking abilities and to step out of the center of discussion. They should allow student-student and student-initiated interaction to take place, yet remain involved to guide the interactive process. Students, conversely, must be willing to participate in the thinking process, tolerate ambiguity, and listen with an open mind before any resolutions are proposed. These and other student and teacher "dispositions," as recognized by Beyer (1987), are discussed in Chapter 2.

A primary rationale in choosing curricula, determining methodology, and creating a compatible classroom climate should be the goal of capitalizing on the young adolescent's developing "capacity for active, engaged thinking . . . to assimilate knowledge . . . challenge the reliability of evidence, or ideas presented; see relationships between ideas; and to ask what-if and suppose-that questions" (Carnegie Council on Adolescent Development, 1989, p. 43). With the approaching advent of a new century, American educators are more mindful of changes that must be made in classrooms to stay abreast with the skills needed to function productively in a global society vastly different from the present. These changes are critically important at this middle level of schooling when students are becoming developmentally ready (and eager) to try out newly discovered cognitive skills. Teaching young adolescents how to reason, to support a position logically, to problem solve, to think critically about issues that will continue to affect their lives, is not only a worthy education goal but a necessary one.

Making Classrooms "Safe" for Young Adolescent Thinking

What makes a classroom "safe" for young adolescent thinking? What factors support a learning environment favorable to thinking? What factors restrict? How can a teacher maintain a "thinking momentum"? Why is the nature of classroom interaction a pivotal factor in the thinking development of the young adolescent student in particular? Many of the answers to these questions lie in the basic principles of cognitive theory and young adolescent development. For example, the level of student thinking is limited in a classroom environment in which a dominating teacher allows little interaction. The young adolescent's brain is most optimally stimulated in an environment of support, challenge, and high involvement. Teachers who relinquish the traditional role of information supplier, and consequently "classroom thinker," and allow the opportunity for their students to practice thinking in a "safe" context, can expect student thinking to improve.

Fortunately for teachers of young adolescents, the more sophisticated cognitive research about how students process information, think, and learn has direct application for classroom instruction. One instructional method useful for teachers of this age student is referred to by Jones (1986) as cognitive instruction. This model is based on the premise that students' capacity to learn can be improved significantly by instruction that seeks to build on their existing knowledge base and to strengthen and expand their current repertoire of thinking and learning strategies. Cognitive instruction has an important application with teaching young adolescents who are learning to think more abstractly about new knowledge and attempting to integrate it with prior knowledge and experience. Teachers must assume an active role in helping students make the necessary link between old and new learning. They also must challenge these students to "stretch" mentally by thinking about new learning in different or more complex ways.

Cognitive instruction supports the role of the teacher as instructional decision maker in the classroom. During class discussion, for example, a teacher must make decisions about the level of question to ask a student, how much assistance to give, and what kind of follow-up questions to pose. The teacher's goal is to help the young adolescent student access what has previously been learned, to add to these current knowledge "structures," and to challenge the student to think more critically as the learning becomes strengthened and internalized. The teacher would need to determine informally the current level of the student's thinking and to structure questioning accordingly. The teacher's questioning should help the student relate to, and thus connect cognitively with, new information; the teacher might also ask the student to apply the learning in a different context. In this way, the teacher both assists with and challenges the young adolescent's developing intellectual capability. A structure for the sequencing of teacher questioning is detailed in Chapter 4 with an explanation of the "Safe" questioning taxonomy. Examples are given that illustrate how teachers might sequence questions to maximize student thinking in the areas of language arts, social studies, science, math, and physical education. Examples of sequenced questioning are provided in Chapter 4.

Cognitive instruction and middle school philosophy in addition both emphasize the need for teachers of young adolescents to understand the learning process from a psychological perspective: Anxiety, fear of failure, and teacher recrimination reduce young adolescents' motivation. Meaningful and appropriately challenging intellectual interaction, however, can enhance both the thinking and learning process (Jones, 1986; Schurr, 1989). Developmentally appropriate cognitive instruction provides students with the opportunity to discuss new information openly and relate it to prior knowledge, to verbalize ideas, to respond to questions of varying cognitive levels, and to reflect on their own thinking processes. Strahan (1987), a cognitive psychologist and active proponent of middle school philosophy, emphasized the need for teachers to provide a systematic instructional framework for the young adolescent's developmental progression from concrete experiences to abstraction. Concentrated instruction at this school level can guide these students in the development of the more complex thinking patterns of analysis, reasoning, and evaluation.

A Safe for Thinking classroom environment is congruent with the developmental needs of the young adolescent. With its emphasis on a community of active learning in which teachers and students respect each others' ideas, a "safe" classroom climate is indeed a safe place for young adolescents to grow intellectually. Within this environment students gain more confidence in their thinking abilities. This setting is one defined by meaningful learning activities, real-world projects, group experiences, personal expression, and choice. A Safe for Thinking classroom is a risk free, yet a structured and expectant setting in which the social, intellectual, physical, and emotional needs of young adolescents are met. Opportunities to be creative or to use multiple talents such as musical, artistic, kinesthetic, and dramatic permit young adolescents to explore various modes of learning and personal definition. A mixture of cooperative learning activities and independent projects nurtures these students' need for peer interaction and for individual time to construct a personal identity.

To maintain a Safe for Thinking environment, and thus sustain thinking momentum over a period of time, teachers need to select a variety of active instructional techniques that appeal to and motivate young adolescents. These techniques should hold the interest of this age learner and consistently engage these students in the thinking process. Such learning experiences might include inquiry-based seminars, thematic units, writing workshops, reading responses, structured collaborative learning, simulations, problem solving, debate, presentation, performance, role play, creative dramatics, and civic action projects. These learning opportunities give young adolescents a chance to "try out" expanding cognitive abilities and to develop a healthy sense of personal self.

A Safe for Thinking classroom climate also reflects a profound respect for individual students, regardless of ability, an acceptance of students' ideas, however diverse, and an active involvement of students in the thinking-learning process. Barell (1985) described a teachers' ability to generate trust and open communication, tolerate and encourage individual differences, and engage students in meaningful and challenging learning as a powerful invitation, perhaps the "sine qua non for higher-level thinking" (p. 22). Within this "safe" classroom context, young adolescents feel personal value, are more apt to attempt the "risky business" of thinking, and begin to gain confidence in their developing thinking abilities.

Summary

Teachers of young adolescents today face the task of preparing this generation of student for a new century characterized predominantly by change. To live meaningfully and productively, these students will need to be flexible thinkers and thoughtful decision makers. Communication skills will be important in the professional setting and introspection will be valuable for reflection and self-evaluation. The challenge of creating a Safe for Thinking learning environment is not as difficult as one might imagine. For half a century, cognitive research has been moving toward a clearer understanding of how students learn and think, what instruction best facilitates the process—and what limits it.

Cognitive instruction for young adolescents focuses on individual students' intellectual needs and offers a flexible learning approach that promises to help them to improve thinking abilities. The emphasis placed on the active role of the teacher as facilitator should empower and challenge teachers to translate the new cognitive theories into daily practice. The following questions may serve as a self-evaluative guide:

- Do I encourage discussion about meaningful and relevant issues?
- Do I ask students questions that cause them to think and reason?
- Do students feel encouraged to pose questions or to respond to each others' questions?
- Do students feel comfortable enough to offer an opinion that differs from the teacher's view?
- Do I expect students' viewpoints to be presented logically?
- Do students consider each others' perspectives respectfully?
- Are standards set high enough for what is an acceptable verbal response?

- Do I probe for clarity of expression or deeper levels of thinking?
- Do I give students choices and involve them in meaningful projects?
- Do I assess closely the logic and coherence of their writing or the quality of their products or performances?
- Do I believe all students can develop and improve thinking ability?

Lois Lowry (1993) in her 1994 Newberry Award book, *The Giver*, described a community in which there was no pain or pleasure, no colors or feelings, no creativity, individuality, or freedom of expression. In this society of sameness, daily existence was characterized by acceptance and compliance. No questions were asked, and certainly no critical thinking was allowed. Only 12-year-old Jonas, with his precocious intellect and tenacity, through the guidance of a wise mentor, was able to break free, and in the process becomes the spiritual hero for a generation of young adolescent readers. A parallel can be drawn between Jonas and his indomitable spirit and the questioning, restless, and ever-changing young adolescent student. Given the opportunity, through thoughtful instruction and with persistent encouragement, today's young adolescents can develop the thinking ability needed to address the problems of their current and future world.

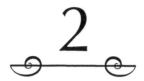

Creating a Safe for Thinking Climate

You see, really and truly, apart from the things anyone can pick up (the dressing and the proper way of speaking and so on), the difference between a lady and a flower girl is not how she behaves but how she's treated. I shall always be a flower girl to Professor Higgins, because he always treats me as a flower girl, and always will; but I know I can be a lady to you, because you always treat me as a lady, and always will.

Eliza Doolittle to Colonel Pickering
Pygmalion, George Bernard Shaw (1940, p. 80)

Overview

Setting the stage for student higher-level thinking does not guarantee it will happen, but the presence of certain positive conditions and the absence of other negative ones precipitate a more favorable and supportive environment. Teachers of young adolescents create a certain climate in the classroom by the way they interact with students—interaction that is frequently influenced by their perception of individual students' abilities. Students, in turn, can form perceptions about their own ability based on how they are treated by teachers. Having the opportunity to respond to more challenging questions or being given time to process information, to elaborate on, or to explain responses can have a positive effect on students' personal feelings about their thinking ability and on their willingness to express this thinking. Teachers should try to establish a classroom climate in which thinking is not only encouraged but anticipated. By extending the opportunity for young adolescent students to participate in higher-level interaction, and expecting them to do so, teachers can lay the foundational groundwork for their thinking development.

Chapter 2 focuses on the feeling and thinking dimensions of a Safe for Thinking classroom climate. These affective and cognitive conditions work in tandem and can be observed through certain classroom interaction patterns. The chapter also describes teacher and student attitudes, or dispositions, that should be in place as prerequisites for a "thoughtful classroom," and those behaviors that indicate when quality thinking is actually happening. The chapter's purpose is to construct a profile of a classroom in which the climate encourages, supports, values, and expects young adolescent thinking to happen and to develop most fully.

Raise Expectations and Extend Opportunities

John Dewey (1933) wrote of a "hidden" curriculum that students learn just by being a member of a classroom. Students may realize, for example, that teachers have the right answer and that they are expected to find it, or they may observe that the teacher is the one who talks and they are expected mainly to listen. "Everything the teacher does, as well as the manner in which he does it, incites the child to respond in some way or other, and each response tends to set the child's attitude in some way or other" (p. 59). Early in their school years, students learn to accommodate what teachers expect. As adolescence approaches, students begin to develop the capacity to think about their own thinking, yet they frequently lack the confidence about their thinking abilities that generally comes as personal identities are established. For these students who are exploring who they are becoming, teachers' actions and expectations can be significant. Unsure of personal abilities and conscious of this uncertainty, young adolescents may begin to form ideas about their thinking capability based on perceived teacher attitudes. These perceptions can affect achievement, academic success, self-concept, and cognitive growth (Strahan, 1987).

Classroom climate, thus, is shaped by the nature and extent of classroom interactions. Consistently judgmental or critical exchanges between teacher and students can have an effect on these students' feelings of self-worth, especially with self-esteem in such a formative stage. A sense of security prevails, however, in the classroom in which students are encouraged to communicate their ideas openly and where these ideas are valued and respected by both teacher and peers. An effective classroom climate, although practically invisible, does not happen by chance: "It is crafted by the artful teacher in subtle but intentional ways" (Marzano, Pickering, & Brandt, 1990, p. 19). Studies have shown that teachers' interpersonal skills have a positive relationship to gains in students' emotional, intellectual, and interpersonal development (Purkey & Novak, 1984).

Because teaching is an interactive process, teachers need to be mindful of the potential effects of classroom interactions on young adolescent behavior, thinking, and learning. Van Hoose and Strahan (1989) urged teachers of this age group to create a climate in which students are willing to risk the uneasy process of thinking by giving opportunities such as problem solving to develop and extend their reasoning potential. If these students experience feelings of frustration because they perceive themselves incapable, they are more likely to construct personal defense mechanisms that may inhibit the thinking process. If limited or negative classroom interaction continues with these students, a cycle of rationalization, that is, "I can't think so I won't try," begins and is perpetuated. Young adolescents need opportunities in a supportive environment to practice and to think about their thinking in positive ways.

Classroom climate is thus affected significantly by the inferences teachers make about students' thinking abilities, and these expectations are communicated through classroom interaction patterns. Unfortunately, studies have indicated that teachers tend to give perceived "low-achieving" students fewer opportunities to express ideas, call on them less, wait less time for them to respond, and ask them fewer higher-level questions (Good & Brophy, 1984). These students obviously receive minimal opportunity for higher-order thinking. Young adolescents are painfully aware of this differential interaction treatment and tend to form lowered self-expectations of personal academic abilities: These students consequently may begin to withdraw from the thinking-learning process.

Teachers can help young adolescents develop their thinking potential if they teach with the assumption that all students can benefit from a thinking-oriented instruction, provided students are given an appropriate opportunity. A primary goal of teaching for thinking is to increase students' confidence in themselves and in their ideas, and to strengthen their ability to do their own thinking. Beyer (1987) offered three guiding assumptions that support the effective teaching of thinking: All students can and do think; all students can think better when guided; and with appropriate instruction, teachers can help all students improve their thinking. Ultimately, the nature of classroom interaction depends on the teachers' beliefs about individual students' thinking abilities and how they convey these expectations to the students. A classroom climate "safe" for thinking is one in which equitable and meaningful opportunities are extended, and where belief, acceptance, and expectation are clearly communicated by teachers to students.

When Thinking Is
Most Likely to Happen

A classroom conducive to the teaching of thinking is not merely psychologically "safe"; its physical makeup, the learning experiences, the curriculum, and particularly, the level of challenge are continual reminders of the long-term expectation for students to think . . . and to learn to think better! Just consider the following scenario: In Toney's seventh-grade classroom, the seating arrangement is flexible to facilitate grouping and face-to-face interaction; students have ready access to a range of resource materials such as paperback and informational books, journals, newspapers, music, videos, databases, Internet and telecommunications; the curriculum materials have meaningful connections to students' lives and interests; and the learning activities give students' choices and options for varied projects and products. Students are motivated and excited because they feel that the learning energy they expend is purposeful and relevant, that Toney values their thinking, and that she is flexible in the ways they can demonstrate their understanding and learning. They also know she expects, and will not accept less than, their best learning performance.

Toney's class reflects a thinking-compatible learning environment in which student activity and student-student interaction occur on a regular basis. Hart (1986) predictably characterized the more traditional classroom, with its rigid physical structure and teacher-dominated learning, as "brain antagonistic." When students are expected to participate, to contribute and consider ideas, to ask questions, to suggest and initiate projects, to make choices, to assume leadership roles, and to evaluate each other and themselves, the brain itself becomes purposefully "engaged" and the thinking capacity begins to flourish. For young adolescents the opportunity to take an active part in classroom activity is consistent with the developmental need to try out newly discovered thinking abilities, to sound out emerging ideas, to ease awkward social skills, and to channel physical energy into constructive learning avenues.

What does a thinking-compatible classroom look like? Steve's language arts classroom may appear in seeming disorder to a passerby, when in actuality it is the scene of a writer's workshop. Initially, Steve might be hard to locate, but with a closer look, he is very much involved in the hub of activity as he monitors progress, reads drafts, and holds conferences with individual students. Working at various stages in the writing process, his students are interested in the topics they have selected and motivated by a sense of ownership, responsibility, and accountability.

Further down the eighth-grade hall, Sara's math students are divided into groups with the task of designing one-dimensional figures directly proportionate to their own bodies. These blueprints will eventually be cut from wood by a parent and dressed by the students in true middle school fashion. A neighboring social studies class, in its study of future communities, is engaged in a seminar discussion about *The Giver* (Lowry, 1993). Students are debating philosophical questions about life without colors, choice, or commitment. Terry's sixth-grade science class has designed hot air balloons to launch on the activity field; on another day they might participate in an edible wildflower "feast" after reading *Hatchet* (Paulsen, 1987). Group discussion, action committees, storytelling, debates, panels, role playing, simulations, and discovery experiments—the options are numerous and limitless. The ground rules, however, remain clear—active involvement in meaningful learning with a high level of challenge.

Attitudes—Theirs and Yours

Over half a century ago, Dewey (1933) entreated teachers to display and encourage in students certain attitudes favorable to the thinking process. These included an "open-mindedness [that] . . . includes an active desire to listen to more sides than one; to heed to facts from whatever source they come; to give full attention to alternate possibilities; to recognize the possibility of error even in the beliefs that are dearest" (p. 30). Beyer (1987), a more recent proponent of critical thinking, has identified a number of similar attitudes or "dispositions that undergird effective thinking." These include (a) a respect for and desire to seek and give reasons, (b) willingness to suspend judgments, (c) a desire to consider other points of view on a topic, (d) a desire to identify and judge a number of alternatives before making a choice, and (e) a willingness to revise one's opinion in light of new evidence (p. 211). Other specialists in the field of critical thinking have collectively emphasized such characteristic "habits of mind" or "intellectual standards" (Ennis, 1987; Paul, 1994).

Young adolescence is a period characterized by a range of thinking levels. Students may enter this developmental period at age 10 or 11 as concrete, egocentric, and rigidly moralistic thinkers; yet they generally progress toward more abstract thinking as they develop the capacity to consider possibilities, examine alternate perspectives, and understand consequences for behaviors. Thirteen-year-olds are considered to be the most "malleable," probably due to the wide variation of reasoning levels within this age group (Scales, 1991). Strahan (1987) observed that approximately one third of eighth graders consistently demonstrate formal reasoning levels.

The message to teachers of young adolescents is twofold: First, there needs to be an attempt to design instruction that will match these students' individual cognitive readiness; and second, there need to be opportunities that will assist students to strengthen emerging thinking abilities as they develop. Teachers might plan, for example, activities that require students to take an alternate stand on an issue or consider the varying perspective of fellow classmates before deciding the best solution to a problem. Accordingly, these teachers are providing practice for their students' budding cognitive abilities, encouraging sociocentric perspectives, and nurturing a receptive mind-set for effective critical thinking.

Beyer (1987) also reasoned that if teachers want to foster the development of thinking attitudes among students, they must themselves model such attitudes. During a class discussion, for example, teachers might seek a variety of viewpoints to open-ended questions or during a problem-solving activity, they require students to consider or develop rationale for a number of possible solutions. Teachers might share reasons for their own decisions or viewpoints, and, in turn, expect similar supporting rationale from students. Most important, if young adolescents are to become increasingly proficient in their thinking ability, their teachers must provide consistent and continuous learning opportunities for students to practice the desired thinking behaviors.

How Challenge Can Motivate

For young adolescent students, challenge is motivational. By their curious, inquisitive, and energetic nature, this age student thrives on challenge that is meaningful, appropriate, and relevant. They love to play with words, to write limericks, to delve into science fiction, to debate political or environmental issues (the more controversial the better), to give opinions, to solve real life problems—the possibilities are endless. These learning experiences challenge and motivate because they engage these students' minds and appeal to their natural interests. Challenge an eighth grader to convert the trial scene of Lee's (1960) *To Kill a Mockingbird* into a drama, perhaps with an alternate finale, or to role play a solution to the problem of the Cherokee Indians' plight along the Trail of Tears. Challenge a group of seventh graders to change the course of events in the science fiction story, *All Summer in a Day* (Bradbury, 1980), or to project what might happen if Laurie's teacher had given his mother a call about Charles's behavior in the popular Shirley Jackson (1951) short story, *Charles*. Likewise, challenge a class of sixth graders to roam the halls as news reporters, uncovering popular "local" opinion on an upcoming student body election. Or, ask them to develop an action plan to make the school lunchroom a more appealing, yet nutritional, place. Challenge means variety, engagement, activity, and involvement. Challenge is not likely to be found in traditional textbook-driven lessons or on worksheets still warm from the school copier.

Challenge is a key ingredient in a Safe for Thinking classroom. It gives young adolescents the freedom to experiment with their imagination, to release their passion for make-believe, to explore their fascination for novelty and fantasy, and to use developing psychomotor skills. Challenge generally sets this age student up for success. Challenge also stimulates the brain's higher-level thinking capacity. Hart's (1986) research showed that the brain is continually active as it works to integrate new experiences and categorize new information with what is already known. The brain is built to be challenged, and students learn best if their limits are stretched and their emotions are engaged. Challenge is motivational and stimulates the mind to make meaning out of learning situations. Challenge directly and meaningfully involves young adolescents in the learning process and contributes to their intellectual growth.

What Does Thinking Look Like?

How does a teacher of young adolescents know when good thinking is actually happening in a classroom? Art Costa (1985), a longtime leader in the thinking skills movement, identified a set of comprehensive thinking behaviors, which he dubbed "what human beings do when they behave intelligently and how they can become more so." These thinking indicators describe the thinking activity of both teachers and students, and reflect the philosophy of cognitive instruction at this grade level. The list of behaviors includes the following:

1. Persisting when solutions to problems are not readily apparent
2. Listening to others with empathy and understanding
3. Checking for accuracy in thinking
4. Questioning and problem solving
5. Drawing on past knowledge and applying it to new situations
6. Metacognition
7. Insightfulness, originality, creativity, flexibility, and inquisitiveness

Teachers of young adolescents need to expect, as well as model, this emphasis on clarity, accuracy, and sensitivity in their effort to create and maintain Safe for Thinking classrooms.

Class discussion serves well to illustrate thinking behaviors in action. One might picture Beth's seventh-grade classroom prior to reading the short story, *The Landlady*, by Roald Dahl (1979). She may read aloud the first few paragraphs in which Billy arrives in London, sets on the quarter-mile walk from the train station to the Bell and Dragon pub. Billy, however, is attracted to a printed notice in the window of a boarding house along his route. Students could be asked to predict subsequent story action, to examine textual clues, and to use their imaginary senses to visualize the late hour and the icy, "deadly" cold temperature of the night air. They might also consider the peculiar manner in which the sign compelled Billy to approach the door of the bed and breakfast establishment and ring the bell. Students would need to draw on past experiences, such as the eeriness of Halloween night, to relate to the foreboding nature of the setting. Certainly, these 12-year-old students' curiosity would be aroused and their predictions prove imaginative and true to the spirit of Dahl's strange tale.

By continuing to read the story in sections and by asking students to make subsequent predictions, teachers would challenge these young adolescents to observe more closely the unfolding foreshadowing, to listen to each others' interpretations, and to remain open-minded and flexible until the story's surprise ending is disclosed and personal speculations are proven or dispelled. Ongoing teacher and student questions could challenge discussion participants to explain the thinking behind predictions and interpretations. Ongoing curiosity about the unfolding events should engage students until the story's conclusion and thinking accuracy is tested. Teacher questioning and verbal interaction are given detailed attention in Chapter 4 when the "Safe" questioning structure is introduced. Sample discussion scenarios are provided to illustrate this questioning-response interplay among students and teacher.

It is apparent that the teacher played an active role in the previous example, and in similar class discussions, not by supplying answers or by critiquing the young adolescents' responses. Rather, the teacher modeled a personal sense of wonderment, posed open-ended and higher-level questions, provided sufficient wait time for students to think, accepted possible responses, redirected questions for alternate interpretations, asked probing questions for clarification and substantiation, and allowed students to ask and answer each others' questions. A "balancing act" effort is required to keep the discussion focused without limiting the flow of student expression. The teachers' purpose is to help students learn *how* to think, not *what* to think. This style of interaction puts the responsibility and accountability for thinking on the student. In addition, teachers need to help young adolescents develop the newly acquired skill of metacognition, as they become aware of personal thought processes and of what indicates active and good thinking.

Adding Enough Rigor to Collaborative Learning

Most readers can readily recall the first day of a new school as a young adolescent. Around the ages of 11 to 12, many young adolescents leave the security of the elementary setting, and tentatively begin a new organizational pattern of schooling. These young adolescents may be confused and frightened by a new physical and social environment that appears large and impersonal. As social awareness develops, these youngsters tend to turn to selected peer groups for a sense of connection. Collaborative grouping is one way teachers can capitalize on the "budding" social tendencies of these young adolescents and help to nurture positive peer relationships. Small groups of learners within a Safe for Thinking classroom can help the young adolescent student become more secure personally and socially. Collaborative grouping can further help them become less egocentric as interpersonal skills are strengthened and they learn to work with peers who may or may not share common viewpoints.

Collaborative learning groups should be structured purposefully for the completion of a meaningful and challenging task. Skills of cooperation, listening, tolerance, respect, consensus building, goal setting, team decision making, follow-through, and evaluation should be expected student behaviors. Even though young adolescents literally live to interact with peers, they are not predisposed to purposeful interaction for the completion of a learning task. Developmentally, these students tend to be competitive, self-centered, argumentative, and often critical of one another. Acquisition of the skills for successful collaborative group work must be taught, expected, monitored, and systematically evaluated by both teacher and individual group members.

Common with other instructional approaches in a Safe for Thinking classroom, collaborative learning opportunities, to be effective for young adolescents, should be thoughtfully designed and clearly communicated. Students should realize what the expected task is, relate to it intellectually and experientially, perceive the social and cognitive behaviors involved for its completion, and understand the evaluative criteria for the end product. (Assessment is discussed in detail in Chapter 5.) The problem to be investigated, the project to be designed, or the experiment to be conducted should capture young adolescents' interests and intrigue by stirring curiosity. They should be motivated to be involved in a task, and committed to the thinking and concerted effort needed for its completion. They should also be aware that the successful completion of the task depends on each person's contribution and positive interdependence among members (Schurr, 1989).

Structuring collaborative learning groups furthermore provides teachers with an excellent opportunity to differentiate for young adolescents' abilities, interests, and talents. Clustering like-ability peers allows teachers to vary the complexity of tasks to match and collectively challenge comparable cognitive abilities. A complex math task involving conceptualization of probability, for example, might be too great a cognitive "jump" for one group of students, yet prove to be an appropriate challenge for another. Clustering students by interest permits a more concerted sharing of common experiences. Clustering heterogeneously opens interaction among students with diverse talents and interests. Young adolescents thus need to be involved in flexible peer groups within the classroom community according to the nature of the task. Teachers need to decide accordingly on which grouping arrangement best "fits" the task and meets their students' cognitive needs.

A look inside Susan's sixth-grade language arts/social studies classroom during an economics lesson illustrates effective collaborative grouping "in action." To understand more concretely the concepts of supply and demand, Susan had grouped students in heterogeneous groups of five. Each group had been given a bag containing a varying assortment of "raw" materials that included colored paper, markers, rulers, scissors, tape, and glue. Each group represented a country with limited natural resources. The task was clearly specified on the overhead: Construct a 12 × 12 inch flag with stripes of 2 alternating colors and 16 stars of a third color arranged in a circular pattern in the top left corner. Ground rules allowed for civil negotiation and trade among groups of countries, if members were in consensus. Completed flags would be inspected according to specified guidelines after a 30-minute work period. Creative approaches to the task were encouraged. The teacher chose not to assign roles within groups.

Group leaders quickly emerged as students assessed resources, planned construction, and made decisions about negotiation options. Creativity emerged as students realized trading meant deciding to give up something of value in the exchange: What a ruler could do, hand estimation could instead approximate. Some students chose to barter for colors of paper or coordinated crayons. The ensuing discussion helped students relate the experience to Third World trade, the implication of embargo negotiation with the Chinese, and the impact of supply and demand on economy and political power. Groups evaluated how effectively members had interacted for the task's duration and individuals made personal decisions about which social skills to improve in subsequent group activities.

On another day, Susan's groups were assembled according to students' interests and special talents. The task was a class production of an original drama of a modern-day reenactment of the Greek mythological story of Pandora. The class, after reading the tale, had generated ideas about present-day evils. They had considered various solutions for a "hopeful" counterbalance to the identified temptations facing today's middle school student. One group was assigned to write the script, another to design the set and suggest costumes for the drama, another to select and tape supporting music, another to formulate a marketing campaign for an afterschool production, and yet another to choreograph the production. Students self-selected the "committees" of interest, an array of options that gave avenues of expression to various talents. A more complete discussion of Gardner's (1983, 1993) theory of multiple intelligences is given in Chapter 3.

On yet another day, Susan used her understanding of flexible grouping in a different formation. She designated "expert" groups for the students to learn about the many facets of social, political, and cultural life in the Peoples' Republic of China. One group's task was to research varying interpretations of the happenings surrounding the events of Tiananmen Square, evaluate in terms of reasons for the different perspectives, and prepare a simulated debate; another group watched a short video on the ancient tradition of foot binding with the task of informing the class in a creative way about this vanishing custom; another was given the assignment to consider and prepare a panel discussion on the pros, cons, and future of the one-child policy; and still another was asked to read a short Chinese fairy tale, compare it to one familiar to them, and prepare a short role play.

Each task was meaningful and each group was appropriately challenged and consequently successful: The thinking required, however, varied in level and complexity. For example, those students asked to examine the events surrounding Tiananmen Square drew on critical thinking that called for analysis, evaluation, and synthesis; this group was composed of higher-ability students with more advanced reading levels. The video interpretation was an appropriate task for students who were more limited readers and better visual learners: They had the opportunity to "stretch" their creative thinking skills through the original presentation. Reading about and assimilating views of the one-child policy involved interpretive thinking of yet another challenge level.

By allowing students of like abilities to be grouped accordingly for certain instructional tasks, Susan was able to use collaborative grouping effectively to differentiate within the mixed-ability classroom. The resulting elevated element of challenge would not have been accomplished as readily through interest-based or randomly formed heterogeneous grouping. In this way, Susan better met the individual and diverse needs of a classroom of young adolescents. Other examples of differentiating for ability and interest are provided in Chapter 6.

The "Safe" Middle-Level Classroom

The entrance to Beth's eighth-grade classroom was decorated to give the appearance of walking into a haunted house. Yes, it was Halloween, but the reason for the festivity was not merely the holiday but the association with the class's current study of *To Kill A Mockingbird* (Lee, 1960). She was counting on the aura of spooks and goblins to set the stage for discussion of the events of Scout and Jem's dark walk home from the school play, costumes in hand, the night of the attack and the surprising rescue. A language arts class? No, but for one period Beth, a math instructor, teaches reading, and the class was well into Lee's novel. The previous day, groups of students had drawn numbers for characters in the novel, given current-day scenarios, and asked to discuss and role play how the assigned character might respond.

Once inside the classroom on this particular day, it became evident, however, that math was the subject of this hour, although the activity was not the traditional teacher-demonstration-of-new-skill followed by student practice. Table desks were arranged by fours to form 2×2 larger square tables. The teams of students faced inward, eyes focused intently on a checkers game board. The problem-solving task was twofold: Student groups were to determine how many squares were on the game board, and then, identify recognizable patterns. Roles had been assigned as task cards were distributed at the start of class: recorder, questioner, reporter, and consensus builder. Students were collaboratively counting small squares and larger squares, soon determining there were sixty-four 1×1 squares, forty-nine 2×2 squares, thirty-six 3×3s, one 8×8—the patterns began to emerge, much to the discernible delight of the student teams. The teacher was circulating, listening to the student discussion, and posing an occasional question to guide or assist the reasoning.

After the groups shared and compared findings and explained their rationale, the teacher proposed, "How many squares would a 10×10 game board have, and why?" She proceeded to ask, "What are other square combinations in real life" (such as tiles, marble floors, Nintendo boards, and so forth)? The ensuing task was to write a challenging word problem using another combination of squares to be solved by another student group. The math skill was geometric patterning, an eighth-grade curriculum objective. The approach was collaborative "hands-on" group problem solving. Students were engaged in active inquiry, responsible for a problem task and its solution. Follow-up activities extended and applied learning to different, although related contexts. The teacher's role was facilitative, not directive; encouraging and expectant, although not controlling. The classroom was a safe place for active student thinking, and active student thinking was evident.

Summary

A teacher's ability to generate trust and to engage young adolescents in meaningful and challenging learning is a powerful invitation. Barell (1985) wrote that without open communication, trust and willingness to acknowledge yet tolerate differences, little thinking can occur. A thinking classroom virtually calls out, "It's okay to think! It's useful to think! Come on, let's learn to think!" (p. 68). Teachers have the power to establish the emotional climate to make young adolescents feel psychologically safe to think and motivated to give thinking the needed effort. A sense of openness that invites students to share unusual ideas and ask unique questions; the freedom to guess, pose hypothetical situations, and make predictions; the opportunity to test ideas, compare, evaluate, examine, and critique; stimulating inquiry; consideration of other students' responses; reward for creative thinking; and time for processing and elaboration are characteristic of a classroom climate "safe" for thinking. Flexible grouping arrangements in which students engage collaboratively in constructive tasks provide practice for the development of important social and cognitive skills. By having high expectations for all students and by placing a strong emphasis on interaction and active learning, teachers of young adolescents can create an accepting and stimulating climate for the development of increasingly complex student thinking.

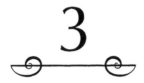

3

Challenging Student Thinking and Learning

It is an inward journey that leads us through time—
forward or back, but seldom in a straight line, most
often spiraling. Each of us is moving, changing,
with respect to others. As we discover, we remember;
remembering, we discover; and most intensely do we
experience this when our separate journeys converge.

One Writer's Beginnings (Eudora Welty, 1984, p. 103)

Thinking is when your mouth shuts up and your head
keeps on talking.

DENNIS THE MENACE
® used by permission of Hank Ketcham and
© by North America Syndicate.

Overview

The early Egyptians held little regard for the human brain,
perceiving it as mysterious matter, useless even for a Pharaoh in his
afterlife existence. Today, the education profession is beginning to

pay considerable attention to brain research and its implication for classroom teaching and learning. Leslie Hart (1986), a leading theorist, pondered, "How can anyone claim that thinking is not a brain function? How can we ignore the incredible organ where thinking occurs?" (p. 46). Related cognitive research has further begun to reshape the long-held concept of intelligence, bringing an enlightened focus on students' multiple abilities (Gardner, 1993). Teachers of young adolescents are currently more aware of strategies that allow these students to learn through kinesthetic, musical, visual, or personal avenues.

Most teachers need to understand better how the brain operates during the thinking and learning process, and teach accordingly (Caine & Caine, 1991; Sylwester, 1995). A common emphasis among these cognitive theorists is the importance of an interactive, challenging, and dynamic learning environment within which students are engaged in meaningful and complex thinking. This chapter presents pertinent findings from current brain research as it applies to the young adolescent. It addresses changing teacher-student relationships and roles within the thinking-responsive classroom, and provides application examples from Gardner's (1983, 1993) theory of multiple intelligences.

The "Inside" Story on Students' Brains

The human brain (yes, even between the ages of 10 and 14!) is staggeringly complex. It links 30 billion intricate nerve cells, or neurons, that interface or connect with trillions of nerve endings, or dendrites, in an elaborate information-processing system. Long nerve fibers, called axons, extend from the cell body and serve as transmitters, sending signals that are picked up by neighboring dendrites. The ends of axons do not actually touch the dendrites of a neighboring cell but chemically transmit information across a region in which the cells are particularly close. The junction is called a synapse, which is believed to be the site for learning and memory. If the nerve pathway is used often, the threshold of the synapse falls and allows the pathway to operate more readily. An increase in the speed of synaptic activity affects students' ability to process information and make learning connections.

A stimulating environment (even for rats!) can affect the growth of dendritic branching, increase the networking among neurons, and increase the number of glial cells, which provide nourishment to the neurons (Caine & Caine, 1991; Hart, 1983). The expression, "I could hear his wheels turning," might be more accurately articulated in these words of one teacher to her eighth graders: "I want to hear your synapses sizzlin'."

The human brain actually consists of three brains, according to the triune brain theory (Hart, 1975). The Reptilian brain, 250 million years old, controls the instincts. The Paleomammalian brain, at the "younger" age of 60 million, is linked to the emotions and is the site of the limbic system. The "newest" brain, at only a few million years old, is the Neomammalian, or cerebrum, and is divided into the left and right hemispheres. Covering 85% or 5/6 of the entire brain area, the cerebrum is the seat of all thinking, learning, and language. Under stressful conditions, such as when a student perceives fear or embarrassment—even meaninglessness, the skittish cerebrum will "downshift" and the limbic system will dominate. In these instances, the emotions will take over and the capacity for thinking is minimized.

The reader may recall personal stressful circumstances when thinking seemed "short-circuited": perhaps as a student reciting a difficult poem from memory under the watchful scrutiny of a judgmental teacher or as an adult relaying disturbing information to a disgruntled and critical group of peers. As a graduate student one might recall the struggle to respond orally to the questions of a professor with a condescending attitude or, as a younger student, the mental "rebellion" at the requirement to memorize a list of 100 state counties.

In a classroom, face-to-face with a dominating or demanding teacher, a young adolescent student might begin to stab at answers, guess haphazardly, or even stutter. Physiologically, the emotion-bound limbic system of the Paleomammalian brain has interfered with the intellectual processing of the cerebrum, and it has become difficult for the student to think beyond immediate recall of information. Access of stored brain information that might help formulate a more complex response is limited. Furthermore, when these students are presented the task of rote memorization without any meaningful context, they may pass the "test" but they tend to forget the information by evening. Little, if any, of what is memorized is internalized into long-term memory.

In a low-risk, yet challenging classroom, however, higher and more complex thinking can happen because the cerebrum can be more fully activated. Caine and Caine (1991) call these ideal conditions for intellectual processing "relaxed alertness," a combination of low threat and high challenge. Both are important: Low threat relaxes the brain whereas high challenge stimulates it. Thinking is regarded as a holistic operation during which the brain encodes information, accesses memory, and works for order and understanding. Challenge excites the whole brain by generating interest and enthusiasm; a readiness for optimal thinking and learning is thus established.

Although students' emotional state (as well as diet, drugs, lack of sleep, and sensory richness) may affect how readily they involve themselves in the thinking and learning process, the level of challenge is also important to their motivational mind-set (Reilly, 1995). Because the brain is continually active, if students are not challenged, if they do not perceive an activity meaningful or relevant or if they can find no way to "connect" the new information to previous learning, they may simply "turnoff," daydream, fantasize, or misbehave. Teachers who insist that students sit passively during a lecture or give assignments that lack complexity, relevance, or value essentially give the young adolescent mind free license to wander.

Although students' brains will continue to develop throughout life, young adolescence is a critical time when cognitive development is more rapid and transformational. Teachers can play an important role in young adolescents' cognitive growth by designing learning experiences that actively and meaningfully challenge socially, emotionally, and intellectually.

How Young Adolescents Learn

Brain theory suggests that the brain is continually attempting to categorize and pattern new information with what it has already learned. At a phenomenally high rate of speed, and apparently in random order on both unconscious and conscious levels, the brain actively integrates and develops what Hart (1983) called "prosters," or program structures. What one knows and thinks about, therefore, changes over time as new experiences and impressions accumulate. Young adolescents learn best when they are able to construct, and consequently reconstruct, personal meaning from experiences that directly involve them. Learning takes place most effectively when they are challenged to " 'call up' the greatest number of appropriate programs, . . . expand on already existing programs, and . . . develop new programs" (Nummela & Rosengren, 1986, p. 50).

Young adolescents naturally vary in the quantity and quality of "program structures" they bring to the learning setting; yet it is the responsibility of teachers to find ways to connect new learning with stored programs, however few or limited. In addition, teachers must try to encourage young adolescent students to become independent learners and thinkers. It is important to teach them how to recall past learning, how to relate it to new circumstances, and how to expand old learning for new understanding. As young adults, these students will need to extract meaning from a stunning quantity of information; thus practice and eventual attainment of these processing skills are critical.

Learning does not happen effectively, however, when young adolescents' experiences are fragmented or isolated, even within what appears to be a rich environment. Learning experiences must be integrative, interactive, and responsive, and students must be actively "immersed." Students' brains develop when they are able to make appropriate connections, as new learning expands, modifies, or changes what is stored in their memories (Caine & Caine, 1991). These students need assistance to "call up" or access previous learning as they try to make sense and impose order on the new. They also need to see connections among many related experiences for a richer and more complex learning structures to form.

As an illustration, consider a marine biology study around the theme of interdependency. In setting the stage, the fifth-grade teacher might ask students to share personal experiences at the coast, to depict these experiences symbolically in a conch shell-shaped coat of arms, and to bring coastal artifacts to class for display in an interactive center. Students could learn about the various ecosystems in coastal waterways by contrasting the adaptation traits of both saltwater and freshwater creatures. Hands-on experiments could be conducted on water salinity, tidal movements, and the simulated effect of saltwater on freshwater fish by using pieces of potato. A saltwater aquarium could be constructed for students to observe directly the interplay of various inhabitants. Students could inspect the anatomy of flounder or flat fish donated by a local fish market. These fish could be painted with tempura for nature prints, as students practiced the ancient Japanese botanist art form of *gyotaku*. The nature prints could then be used to illustrate poetry, creative stories, vocabulary booklets, or informational brochures about marine and coastal life. Ghost stories and myths about early pirating in the inland waterways could be read, written, and dramatized.

These 10-year-olds might dissect squid to observe body movement capability, the digestion system, and self-protection mechanisms. Tiny pieces of ink sacs could be dropped into glasses of water for students to visualize a survival technique, and videos might be watched for the real life interplay of squid and predators. An exotic seafood tasting party would expose students' taste buds to shark, clams, crab, and squid. Ethical dilemmas and issues, such as preservation of the nation's wetlands, could be discussed and debated from differing perspectives. The interdependency theme could be further reinforced by drawing parallels to related issues such as rain forest ecology. A culminating class excursion to a marine center on the coast would be fun, if possible, or at least students could visit a local science center with "touch tanks." Parents would gladly be involved as assistants and consultants.

The important criteria for this thematic unit is the students' active and high-interest involvement and in their ability to make rich connections within a context of multiple and mutually reinforcing learning experiences. Young adolescents' brains are naturally motivated, challenged, and rechallenged as they make meaning from the myriad experiences that support new learning. This setting is "safe" for young adolescent thinking, the brain's capacity is optimized, and long-lasting learning is more likely to occur.

The Thinking-Learning Connection

In a popular cartoon a few years ago, a young character lamented to his older companion that he had difficulty in school remembering information from one test to the other, and that he totally forgot everything over the summer. He questioned what he would have "left" when he graduated. The wise elder ventured, "An education." Students and educators are familiar with the "brain-drain" dilemma. Although the mind rarely forgets, the ability to access previous learning is sometimes limited, especially when old "learning" was memorized or acquired in isolated, unrelated factual fragments.

Although immediate test scores might reflect success, the bits of learning are not meaningfully connected within the brain's stored program structures. This lack of substantial and meaningful connection might explain the young character's dilemma.

Teachers are held accountable for student performance on tests, many of which are constructed for factual recall of course content. This pressure may explain why many teachers push for the quick absorption of pieces of information. For students who memorize well and recall quickly, this approach may work; unfortunately, many students find such a learning task difficult, painstaking, and failure inviting. Students need time to make meaningful connections, to think about learning in a variety of contexts, and to put some sort of mental order to it if it is to be internalized. Learning in this way forms stronger and more complex "prosters" that can be accessed more readily and expanded as learning continues.

Experiences in classrooms can be the catalyst for more integrated and lasting learning. These learning experiences should purposefully excite the senses, challenge thinking, and captivate interest; they should also use a range of talent, incorporate physical movement, and involve social interaction. A tall order for teachers of the 10- to 14-year-old student! The payoff—learning, nevertheless, is what education is supposedly about. This learning is of the long-term variety associated with cognitive instruction and Safe for Thinking classrooms. And this learning is the kind that is developmentally responsive to the social, intellectual, physical, moral, and psychological needs of the young adolescent.

In their book, *Raising Self-Reliant Children in a Self-Indulgent World*, Glenn and Nelson (1991) projected that by the time current kindergartners are ready for graduation, the amount of accessible information in the world will be increasing at a rate of 200% monthly. Teachers cannot expect to "teach it all." Decisions about what to teach can no longer be determined by a set body of content knowledge. Teachers of young adolescents instead will have to determine what content best integrates with the interests and experiences of their students. These criteria do not mean the elimination of long-revered classics from school curricula. They do mean that decisions to teach certain content should be based, not on what has "always been taught" or what interests teachers but on what relates to the lives of the students. Young adolescents need to know how to think meaningfully and purposefully about issues that affect them; how to develop the capacity to verbalize, write, or artistically express their thinking; and how to use skills of inquiry, reasoning, and decision making to direct future learning patterns.

The New View of Intelligence

A local middle school was the scene of media attention a couple of years ago. After reading *The Pushcart War* (Merrill, 1978) in language arts class, 37 seventh graders turned the schools' hallways into a replica of New York's famous Delancey Street. Teams of students sold candy, flowers, tools, and other marketable items from homemade pushcarts. Designs for the carts had been discussed by teams of students, drawn to scale, constructed, and decorated. The real test had been the "publication," or, in this case, the successful operation of the pushcarts by the student vendors in the school's market of peers. Students also wrote creatively about the experience, which was an integrated learning project between the middle school and a local university. Both schools were interested in the practical application of Howard Gardner's (1983) *Theory of Multiple Intelligences.* Gardner's early research at Harvard University's Project Zero proposed a view of intelligence as multidimensional and the product of both individual and cultural factors. Gardner's theory proposed that there are at least seven intelligences: verbal-linguistic, logical-mathematical, visual-spatial, bodily-kinesthetic, musical-rhythmic, interpersonal, and intrapersonal.

The traditional instructional practices of American schools have tended to limit how students learn and are evaluated to the spoken and written word (verbal-linguistic) or to structured problem-solving approaches that require logical-mathematical thinking. Understandably, for many teachers the Pushcart War project would be a major undertaking: The concept of multiple intelligence theory, however, can be incorporated into daily instruction in a variety of manageable ways. Teachers can expand and vary students' learning opportunities to include artistic and musical exploration, group interaction, "hands-on" experimentation, simulation, and dramatics.

In a study of Native American culture, for example, students might listen to ancient legends and adapt them to life in the present century (verbal-linguistic). They could identify and debate social issues that impact on current cross-cultural relationships (logical-mathematical/verbal-linguistic) or group problem solve through a reenactment of the historical Trail of Tears saga (interpersonal/bodily-kinesthetic). Students could construct masks to reflect their own personalities (visual-spatial/intrapersonal) or compose songs to convey ancient tribal customs (verbal-linguistic-musical-rhythmic). They could design symbolic alphabets, create dances, write messages, re-tell stories, graph population growth or fashion personal totem poles, shields and medicine pouches (Maker, Nielson, & Rogers, 1994).

Through multiple instructional approaches such as these, young adolescents can explore various strengths and interests, and as a result, find new avenues for successful learning. These varied approaches could also help teachers respond to students with diverse cultural and linguistic needs.

The implications of multiple intelligences (MI) theory for thinking instruction are strong. First, the theory heralds diversity among young adolescent learners and calls for differing instructional approaches for differing intellectual needs. Students are given choices by which to process information and construct meaning from experiences designed in response to their learning needs and strengths (Reilly, 1995). These young adolescents can thus explore, discover, and determine how best they learn. MI theory also supports an integrative approach to instructional practice that is developmentally appropriate for young adolescents. These students need and are motivated by the opportunity to explore and learn about themselves in an action-oriented setting.

Verbal-linguistic intelligence can be expressed through storytelling, journal writing, "far-out" vocabulary terms, debates, editorial writing, and the creation of witty captions for political cartoons. Logical-mathematical talent can be explored by solving mysteries or puzzles, through deductive reasoning, by conducting scientific investigations around self-initiated hypotheses, or by discerning relationships and patterns in tessellations. Visual-spatial intelligence can find catalyst through artistic media such as paint, clay, pens, markers, or sculpture. It can be incorporated into the study of photosynthesis, for example, by having students visualize, then draw the steps of an imaginary journey inside the cell factory of a green leaf, or with mind maps that depict the important concepts of a passage of historical text (Lazear, 1991).

Exploring body-kinesthetic intelligence is a natural for young adolescents who so willingly use their bodies to express emotion and thrive on the accompanying energy release. Students can reenact events in history, learn vocabulary kinesthetically, or discipline body movement through creative dramatics. Young adolescents' interest in music opens a path for rhythmic expression. Songs can be composed to assist learning or to illustrate a story's action or theme; and tapes of various nature sounds (ocean waves, a rain forest, a hurricane) can be played for relaxation, creative writing, or as motivation for a discussion of natural patterns and rhythms.

Interpersonal and intrapersonal intelligence can be nurtured through structured group activities in which students work collaboratively to solve a problem or complete a project. The young adolescents who worked together to design, construct, and successfully operate the pushcarts in the opening example had to use interpersonal skills to make progress in the task, and likely for some, peer cooperation and tolerance came more readily! Roles assigned in cooperative learning activities can provide students with needed practice in the social skills of consensus building, collaboration, and leadership. A few questions that might guide teachers (Armstrong, 1994, p. 58) as they plan multiple intelligences follow:

- How have I planned for students to speak or write?
- How have I incorporated logic, calculation, and critical thinking?
- How have I used visualization, art, and color?
- How have I used music, environmental sounds, or a melodic framework?
- How have I involved body movement and hands-on experience?
- How have I planned for peer sharing or collaborative interaction?
- How have I helped students think about personal feelings or thinking?

Of key importance for young adolescents is the emphasis of MI theory on the personal skills of introspection, reflection, and metacognition. Students in this age group are daily negotiating self-identities as they explore a range of emotions and perceptions mirrored by the world around them. Writing in journals, plotting moods, discerning anxiety patterns, identifying thought patterns for personal decisions, and projecting about the future are learning experiences that involve young adolescents actively in the development of a healthy sense of self.

Chapter 6 provides additional examples of products that show how teachers might adapt Gardner's MI Theory meaningfully to classroom learning experiences, and Chapter 5 offers suggestions for product evaluation and learning assessment. Through multiple instructional approaches and product development, young adolescents can explore various strengths and interests, and as a result, find new avenues for successful learning. Varied approaches also help teachers respond to students with diverse cultural, linguistic, and nontraditional learning needs. The sixth-grade science scenario at the end of this chapter further illustrates Gardner's MI Theory adapted into practice.

Cognitive Development and the Young Adolescent

Young adolescent students display a wide range of cognitive ability as their minds traverse the "thinking terrain" between concrete and the capacity for abstract thought. In *Dynamite in the Classroom*, Schurr (1989, p. 23) described this intellectual passage as rendering the capacity for the following:

1. Propositional thinking

2. Hypothetical reasoning and deduction

3. Interpretation of symbols, concepts, themes, sayings, and generalizations

4. Insight into previously unquestioned values, attitudes, or behaviors

5. Appreciation of mathematical logic

6. Analysis of political ideology

7. Understanding of the nuances of poetic metaphor and musical notation

8. Ability to project thought into the future

Intellectual development also unleashes in young adolescents an intense curiosity and a drive to know about things that interest or fascinate them. Science fiction, mystery, death, and the macabre are such examples. These students are keenly independent in their thinking but prefer to work with friends in a learning situation. They are forming values but tend to hold fast to a strict moral code of right and wrong (which often causes them to be critical and judgmental). And for the first time in their lives, they have the metacognitive capacity to think about their own thinking and thinking ability. Even so, academic goals remain secondary to the personal and social concerns that dominate their thought and activity.

How can teachers deal with the varied and changing state of young adolescence? A parent, in describing her son's eighth-grade teacher, said, "He's real. He shows them he's one of them." Certainly, this mother did not mean that the teacher was reliving his own adolescence! (For that matter, who would want to?) What she was attempting to convey is that this eighth-grade teacher understood what it was like to be 13 years old. Honored by the school system for outstanding teaching performance, this young man admitted in a conversation that he sometimes felt discouraged with the unpredictability of the early adolescent nature. He daily dealt with the "ups and downs," the mood swings, the emotional backlashes intended to cut, and the disappointing bad-judgment mistakes of his eighth-grade students. He reasoned that teachers of young adolescents must continually seek and maintain perspective; for they, if respected, can be a significant influence on the direction of these students' lives. He takes his job seriously, and his classroom is a "safe" place for students to develop their thinking skills.

Once, in a discussion of *Flowers for Algernon* (Keyes, 1959), this popular language arts teacher asked students if they felt that Charley should have been given the experimental drug to expand his mental ability. Thirteen-year-olds pondered and discussed what it would be like not to be able to have and use intellectual skills, and if it is ethical to tamper chemically with intelligence. In a later discussion of the novel *The Giver* (Lowry, 1993), the students wrestled with another ethical dilemma: whether giving up one's freedom of choice and decision making is an equal trade for the absence of pain or physical discomfort. They were asked to speculate what it would be like to be an eighth grader in a world with no color, or cold, or worry. When one student questioned what the author meant by "stirrings," this teacher calmly and directly explained Lowry's reference to sexual arousal, which was soon to be controlled with a pill. More astute classmates stifled smiles and exchanged looks but did not comment. Acceptance was the tone of the discussion, as was high-level engagement. In another instance, students were asked to draw parallels between their own culture and that presented in a popular screen allegory about adolescent turtles. In addition, they were asked to determine and critique the film's message in terms of their own lives.

The cognitive development of young adolescents depends on these kinds of "real" learning experiences. In the previous examples, students were challenged to stretch their cognitive capacities as they considered issues relevant to their current and future lives, and to make sense from textual interpretation. In a context in which their ideas were valued and thinking behaviors were modeled by the teacher, students entered without hesitation into the inquiry, responded actively, and questioned to make meaning from the learning. In this "safe" context, day by day, young adolescents will develop and refine their intellectual skills, and grow into mature young adults.

The "Thinking-Responsive" Middle-Level Classroom

Kerrie's sixth-grade science "class-lab" was a hub of activity. Students were clustered in fours and fives around station tables, busy with the assigned task of predicting the number and assortment of colors of M & M® candies in a one-pound bag based on the information given on the outside of the bag. Students were reading about volume and serving size, measuring, weighing, and hypothesizing. Once predictions were recorded, students continued with estimations for the number of each color and predicted ratios for the projected bag composition. They had also been asked to discuss other questions: How many servings (or bags) of caloric intake would it take for a "couch potato" to gain one pound? What is the percentage of saturated fat per serving? How might they justify an active 11-year-old eating M&Ms®? What would be a reasonable intake? Kerrie also teaches the students math, but on most days, it is difficult to separate disciplines.

The next step in the scientific method tested the hypotheses as students carefully opened the bags and counted and categorized the candy by color. Two students began entering the actual data on one of the class computers, using a familiar statistics package to generate both pie and bar graphs (in color). The remaining two or three students began generating ideas that would explain discrepancies between predicted hypotheses and actual findings. For example, is one color better liked by the American market? Is the color combination systematic or random? Of course, these students immediately compared findings with other groups. From this speculation conclusions were drawn and posted with the computer-generated graphs on the research bulletin board titled, "Calculating Candy and Other Consumer Concerns." Of course, they were given the candy to eat . . . after agreeing to take a neighborhood walk after school instead of watching TV.

The final group task, assigned over subsequent days, was to create an advertising campaign for a new color of M&Ms® that would appeal to the middle school consumer market. An actual vote would be taken by the student body, with the winning suggestion sent to Nabisco®. Discussion of colors ranged from those associated with popular sports teams to more creative color combinations, such as bubble gum pink, razzlin' raspberry, alternative orange, patriotic pinstripe. The class critiqued ads cut from teen magazines and videotaped from MTV®, and discussed advertising and campaign ethics. Journal response writing profiled what students regarded as advertising integrity.

Ensuing work on the advertising campaigns progressed into subsequent days and involved the collaboration of Kerrie's teammate whose specialty area is language arts-social studies. Student teams generated slogans, posters, banners, and flyers to be posted and distributed around the school. One group used wax crayons to draw iron-on logos, which they sported on tee shirts on voting day. Another team wrote a musical video, which the principal allowed to be programmed following morning announcements. Group members campaigned actively among the student population before and after school. Roaming reporters kept abreast of "public" opinion, projecting an informal poll from samples of students at various grade levels. The class discussed why certain campaign strategies (or colors) might appeal to certain age populations, and if any gender representation in the samples factored into preference, and why. Similar analyses were done with the actual results of the student body vote.

Kerrie's class reflects active, student-centered learning and a thinking-responsive setting. Students are using skills of experimentation, analysis, prediction, testing assumptions, reasoning, planning, and synthesis, to name a few, in a setting of high challenge and structured expectation. They are interacting with peers within both classroom and school, and are physically mobile. They are dealing with familiar and interesting subject matter—candy and marketing within the middle school population, and building on and expanding this knowledge base. They have the freedom to use creative and multiple talents, yet ethical and strategic marketing are clearly communicated as product criteria. These young adolescents' minds are actively engaged in a task of high interest, and an understanding of the "science" of consumer marketing is reinforced through interdisciplinary study. In addition, Kerrie's class represents an application of multiple intelligence theory. Students collaborate in groups as they conduct scientific inquiry, calculate, problem solve, and plan advertising campaigns. They have options for musical, artistic, and kinesthetic expression, practice the verbal skills of salesmanship, and discuss campaign ethics that encourage self-reflection and team monitoring. The learning opportunities are multiple, integrative, and reinforcing, and one might venture, Kerrie's young adolescents will remember the experience for years to come.

Summary

Teaching for thinking pays attention to how young adolescents learn. An emerging field of cognitive science has provided valuable insight into how the brain functions in the thinking and learning process; the conditions that contribute or limit; and the impact of a dynamic, interactive, challenging, and supportive environment on the process and on intellectual development. The implications for classroom practice with young adolescents are clear and timely: Instruction must be relevant and integrative; students need help to make meaningful, multiple, and increasingly complex learning connections; and their minds must be challenged to participate actively in the thinking and learning process.

Teachers' roles and responsibilities in this interactive process are of particular importance. Teachers of young adolescents are critical decision makers who are challenged to plan and implement instruction that is responsive to developing minds. The theory of multiple intelligences (Gardner, 1983, 1993) expands learning and thinking options in the classroom, and has the potential for adding instructional variety and for increasing students' opportunities for success. The renaissance mind of young adolescents cognitively celebrates meaningful and challenging learning experiences in thinking-expectant settings.

4

Interacting Through Questioning and Inquiry

Yesterday I knew all the answers
Or I knew my parents did.
Yesterday I had my Best Friend
And my Second Best Friend
And I knew whose Best Friend I was
And who disliked me.
Yesterday I hated asparagus and coconut and parsnips
And mustard pickles and olives
And anything else I'd never tasted.
Yesterday I knew what was Right and what was Wrong
And I never had any trouble deciding which was which.
It always seemed so obvious.
But today . . . everything's changing.
I suddenly have a million unanswered questions.
Everybody I meet might become a friend.
I tried eating snails with garlic sauce—and I liked them!
And I know the delicate shadings that lie between
Good and evil—and I face their dilemma.
Life is harder now . . . and yet, easier . . .
And more and more exciting.

> *Yesterday, "Hey world, here I am!"* (© 1986, Jean Little,
> used with permission)

Overview

As Kate resounds in this opening poem, young adolescents have "a million unanswered questions" as they tentatively negotiate the passage through this period of development. They are beginning to see that gray areas and "delicate shadings" matter, and that choices between right and wrong are not always clear-cut. They face the disillusioning realization that life is not always fair and that even heroes have flaws. They want to try on a thousand identities, yet they hesitate to differ from their peer group. They are motivated to talk about problems and issues as they seek a more complex and complete understanding of their world and of human nature. For the first time they are concerned about the future, their appearance, and the opposite sex—usually in the same thought sequence. The time is right for inquiry-based instruction.

Chapter 4 focuses on inquiry-oriented interaction among teachers and young adolescent students during classroom discussion. Teacher questioning is presented as an instructional tool to stimulate student cognitive processing and learning. A "Safe" taxonomy (Beamon, 1990, 1992-1993) is offered as a guide for the formulation of questions by cognitive level. The "Safe" model is grounded in cognitive research and designed to help students make meaningful connections with and think with increasing complexity about new information. A priority of Chapter 4 is to familiarize educators with specific questioning strategies that sequence cognitive level and process according to young adolescents' learning needs. When used in an interactive and supportive setting, these questioning techniques can help these students formulate their thoughts and improve the quality of their thinking expression.

The Power of Teacher Questioning

Over 2,000 years ago, Socrates artfully and purposefully sequenced questions to guide his students to discover new knowledge. In classrooms today, questioning remains a powerful instructional tool to enhance the intellectual development of the early adolescent (Schurr, 1989). Teachers can strategically use questioning to stimulate young adolescent thinking by posing questions at different cognitive levels, probing and challenging with clarification and follow-up questions, and encouraging students to ask questions themselves. Questioning techniques that elicit critical thinking ask students to explain a point of view, to give reasons or evidence for a viewpoint, and to offer alternate ways of looking at a particular claim. Often called Socratic questioning, this process probes students' thinking more deeply and requires that they justify their responses. As students become more skillful with the critical thinking process, they will become more intrinsically inclined to seek reasons and evidence, to suspend judgment, and to examine issues from differing perspectives (Ennis, 1987; Paul, 1994).

The teacher who controls classroom discourse by asking a series of questions in a fast-paced interchange, however, does little to encourage higher-level thinking among young adolescent learners. Consider the following seventh-grade language arts classroom as the scene of such a controlled "discussion." The teacher has in hand a list of 30-some questions about a short story the students have read. She proceeds to "fire" these predominately knowledge-level questions in rapid succession, making certain that the 30-some students all have an opportunity to respond. The teacher obviously knows the answers she is seeking, and in most cases, so do the students. No time is given for students to expound on their ideas or to ask their own questions. In fact, most of the questions can be so readily answered that the need for extended thinking or wait time is unnecessary. The teacher asks a few analysis level questions but offers no follow-up questioning that seeks reasons for students' interpretation. No questions are redirected for alternate opinions. Such a question-answer exchange with the teacher as the "superordinate partner," does little to stimulate thinking; the discourse will, however, encourage students to be dependent and passive (Dillon, 1981, p. 51). As students become conditioned to a minimal response expectation, the classroom dialogue will become more that of recitation than discussion.

If, on the other hand, teachers want to foster a climate of inquiry among young adolescents, they need to talk less, ask more higher-level questions, and ask more interpretive, or what Dillon (1981) has called "perplexing" questions. Students are thereby given the chance to respond to intriguing questions that invite thought and elaboration. Strother (1989) suggested that teachers who have a particular reason for asking a question, who listen to students' answers, and who shape their follow-up responses and questions accordingly are more apt to enhance student understanding. Teachers who redirect questions for clarification or verification, furthermore, challenge young adolescent students to be less impulsive and more accountable for their thinking expression: They will soon begin to realize that they are expected to think more carefully about ideas before responses are given.

In addition, because young adolescents are beginning to develop metacognitive skills, or the capacity to think about their own thinking, they will be able to respond to questions that encourage them to examine their own thought processes. Referred to as "reflexive thinking" by Van Hoose and Strahan (1989), this cognitive skill enables young adolescents to be more aware of the level and quality of their thinking expression. They can begin to develop the capacity to reflect on and evaluate personal ideas and thinking articulation. Also, because young adolescents tend to be overly self-critical and self-conscious about others' perceptions of their developing capacity to think in a "new key" (Elkind, 1984), they need to feel that their ideas are worthy. In a Safe for Thinking setting, these students feel that their thinking expression is supported and valued. Teachers, therefore, should create a climate of inquiry in which young adolescents' tentative thinking expression is nurtured, challenged, and, through practice, strengthened.

Getting All Students to Answer

Young adolescents may have "a million unanswered questions," yet some are reluctant to ask them in the social context of class discussion. They may hesitate to volunteer answers for fear of being incorrect, or they do not want to risk appearing too "intellectual" to members of the opposite gender. Others may be unaccustomed to rendering anything beyond brief or "half thought-out" responses. Others may not have cognitively grasped the more subtle meaning of a passage and thus struggle with interpretive questions. Still others may have had limited previous experience with inquiry-oriented questioning or with a teacher's expectation for more thoughtful verbal responses. Some students, conversely, may revel in the opportunity to appear knowledgeable and tend to dominate a discussion.

Various developmental and experiential influences may shape young adolescents' willingness and ability to participate in class discussion, yet their teachers need to encourage and assist all to be involved. Familiarity with basic questioning-response techniques can help teachers guide class discussion and help students improve thinking skills. Consider the following eighth-grade language arts classroom as contrast to the previous illustration:

Amanda's students had read Kurt Vonnegut's (1968) *Harrison Bergeron* for homework. Prior to class, she had formulated questions, but instead of a series of seemingly unrelated ones, she had chosen a few broad, pivotal questions that she hoped would promote student thinking. In structuring the questions, Amanda considered cognitive level, experiences familiar to her students, and the questions' relevance to contemporary issues of interest. This teacher's goal was to guide but not control student thinking: She was mindful that the questions be open-ended and reflective of her own curiosity. For example, Amanda wondered what her students' reaction would be to a society in which all competition by ability was eliminated. Did students agree that people should be "equalized" for equal opportunity, much like a golf handicap? Was being "equalized" equivalent to equal opportunity for all? How did they personally relate to the idea of "equalization" as eighth graders? Could relationships be improved, for example, if no student were allowed to dress better or look prettier or appear brighter? Could they draw parallels between the Handicapper General and the regulating leadership in *The Giver*, (Lowry, 1993) read earlier in the semester? Students had also been asked to write their own questions regarding the story, which would be added to the class discussion.

Amanda opened the discussion by posing a question to the entire class before calling on a particular student. Her intent was for all students to respond mentally, as well as convey the expectancy that any of them could be called on to answer. During the course of the discussion, Amanda called on both volunteers and nonvolunteers, varied the phrasing of a question if it seemed unclear to a student, and paused before and after the students' responses. She also skillfully used students' correct answers to determine follow-up questions. At times, Amanda referred students' answers or questions to other students for response.

Amanda avoided agreeing or disagreeing with students' responses. She purposefully withheld her personal viewpoint so as not to influence students' thinking. She often asked students to elaborate on ideas, to explain a point of view, and to provide clues that had helped them formulate their perspective. She paraphrased students' answers, rather than repeating them. She accepted students' ideas, invited additional contributions, and urged them to pose their own questions. If a student had difficulty with a higher-level question, Amanda asked one or two less complex ones to be sure the student understood the basic information: She then re-asked the original.

Students responded well to Amanda's questioning techniques. They discussed both the negative and positive sides of popularity and student cliques. Most defended the right of individual choice but struggled with the notion of equal opportunity. They were asked to give examples from present society, other than on the golf course, in which "conditions" appeared to be equalized for equal opportunity. Did they consider equalization fair to those with superior abilities? Should all people, regardless of ability, be given an even chance? in sports? in academics? in cultural arts?

Through this guided questioning, some students began to build a case for diversity and individual talent. Most began to distinguish between situations in which "handicapping" functioned positively to equalize opportunity and other times when the condition would stifle the individual freedom to excel. Students also talked about abstract notions such as tolerance, acceptance, and celebration of individuality, and the humane treatment of others.

In this illustration, interaction remained high because the discussion was relevant and meaningful to the students. The teacher's skillful use of questioning helped students see connections among previous knowledge, personal experiences, and new, more abstract ideas. Even the most reluctant students felt encouraged (and expected) to participate and were able to make sense of Vonnegut's allegory. These students were motivated by the pertinent issues discussed and the interpretive questions asked; they were also motivated by the recognizable expectancy, challenge, and acceptance within the class as a learning community. Within this "safe" context, these young adolescents were able to test new ways of thinking and understand better the "delicate shadings" of more formal thought. A few summarizing ideas help explain why the thinking level in some discussions never "gets off the ground"!

- The topic might be beyond students' interest, knowledge, or experience.
- The topic is not relevant to them.
- Students feel ridicule or disapproval.
- The questions either are too obvious or too difficult.
- The teacher talks too much and likes to answer his or her own questions.
- The teacher is dogmatic, unfair, or intolerant.
- The thinking does not go deep enough to challenge.
- The questions are not clear or leading.
- The discussion is dominated by one person who "knows it all."
- The discussion of one point becomes worn out.
- Argument and debate take the place of group thinking.

How to Construct "Safe" Questions

Students' background experiences and previous learning opportunities influence, according to Hart (1983), the number and complexity of students' program structures. For young adolescents, learning and thinking readiness also varies developmentally as new, complex thinking routes are charted within the brain. Some students, perhaps from less advantaged backgrounds, may have difficulty responding to higher-order questions because they lack the supporting knowledge base (Gall, 1984). Teachers thus should try to structure questions for two purposes: to help students arrive at a basic understanding of new information and to help them to think about the new learning with more depth. Young adolescents who are just beginning to think abstractly need the concrete "building" of lower-level questions and the "stretch power" of higher-level ones. The purposeful

Setting Up the Knowledge Base
Do students remember the facts?
Do they understand the meaning?
Do they make the relevant connections?
Can they connect with previous learning?
Can they relate through experiences?

Analyzing the New Knowledge
Do they see relationships among events?
Can they make inferences based on facts?
Can they compare with old knowledge?
Can they interpret or explain?
Can they categorize? classify?
Can they distinguish fact from fiction?

Focusing the New Knowledge
Can they make predictions about?
Can they focus knowledge in a different direction?
Can they think of another way to?
Can they adapt to a new situation?
Can they make a hypothesis about?

Evaluating the New Knowledge
Can they give an opinion or a critique?
Can they judge? debate?
Can they appraise against criteria?
Can they give value to?

Figure 4.1. Cognitive Level of Questions
SOURCE: © Beamon (1990).

sequencing of questions helps students relate new learning with the knowledge and experiences they bring to the learning experience.

The "Safe" question classification model (Beamon, 1990) was designed to help teachers of young adolescents to formulate questions on four cognitive levels (see Figure 4.1). Teachers can purposefully sequence the questioning levels to help students make basic and meaningful connections with new knowledge and to begin to think about new learning in a more complex manner.

The first cognitive level of the "Safe" model is Setting Up the Knowledge Base (S level), a classification of questions whereby students are asked to remember facts, relate personal experience, and make meaningful concrete connections with new knowledge. These are literal questions, and the answers are usually apparent.

The next level, Analyzing the New Knowledge (A level), classifies questions that ask students to make inferences, to interpret information based on contextual clues, to compare or explain, and to see relationships within the new learning context. To respond to these questions, students need to analyze textual clues to arrive at understanding.

The Focusing the New Knowledge (F level) is characterized by questions that encourage divergent thinking as students are asked to make predictions, to hypothesize, to synthesize, or to adapt learning to a new situation or in a new direction.

The fourth cognitive level, Evaluating the New Knowledge (E level), classifies questions that require students to evaluatively judge, appraise, critique, or give personal value to new knowledge.

To illustrate the "Safe" classification scheme, consider the familiar tale of *Jack and the Beanstalk* (Johnson, 1976); S-level questions might include the following:

- What was Jack's purpose for climbing up the beanstalk the first time?
- Did Jack plan to steal from the giant when he climbed the beanstalk the first time?
- Have you ever been tempted to follow a pathway up a wooded hill out of sheer curiosity?
- How did the giant know a stranger was present?

Responses to these factual questions can be readily supplied as students examine the reading or reflect on personal experiences. They are useful for teachers to find out students' foundational level of content understanding and help them make experiential connections.

A-level questions might include the following:

- Does the author want you to believe that the man who gave Jack the beans is trying to help Jack or take advantage of him?
- Why did the giant's wife try to keep Jack from being eaten on his first trip up the beanstalk?
- Why does Jack go up the beanstalk a third time?

To respond to these analysis-level questions, students must examine contributing textual clues and venture an interpretation. Responses may vary and students need a chance to justify a particular line of thinking by drawing reference to textual indicators.

F-level questions might ask students to hypothesize what sort of life Jack would have had if he had not sold his mother's cow for the beans, or to speculate how the story might have changed had Jack not gone up the beanstalk a third time. These questions should not encourage wild guessing among students; rather, F-level questions are designed to encourage logical predictions based on interpretation of actual story events and character motivation analysis.

E-level questions require students to apply internal criteria for right and wrong to a situation or a character's action after having considered contributing reasons or motivation. This level is a complex thinking task for young adolescents who are forming personal value systems. The following are examples:

* Would you have exchanged the cow for the old man's beans?
* Do you think Jack was wrong for going up the beanstalk a third time?
* Does your mother's approval of what you do become less important as you get older?

In a social studies discussion about the lifestyle and traditions of the great Maasai tribe of Kenya, Joy wanted her sixth-grade students to become aware of a west African culture distinctly different from their own, to understand why and how this fascinating culture has been preserved, and to recognize parallels within their own society. S-level questions included the following:

* What characterizes the physical features of the Rift Valley plateaus where the Maasai settled?
* What is meant by the "steppes of the Maasai"?
* What are some of the unique customs of the Maasai?
* How do the Maasai regard children? cows? other animals? the elderly?
* Why do the Maasai people paint their bodies?

* Why do they decorate their bodies with beads and other ornamentation?
* How do the Maasai govern themselves?
* Why have the Samburu tribes been given the name of "butterflies"?
* Are present-day Maasai a warring or peaceful people?

The purpose of these S-level questions is to help students construct and relate to new knowledge about the Maasai tribes.

Joy asked A-level questions to help students think about the new information in an interpretive manner:

* How do the Maasai hair-cutting ceremonies compare with American beauty salons or barber shops?
* Are there other customs that are similar to any in our society?
* What is the significance of the color red?
* Why do the Maasai place such high value on age groups?
* Why have the Maasai remained isolated from the more advanced cultures of western Africa?
* How have the Maasai been able to preserve their ancient traditions?

F-level questions should challenge students to think divergently about the new information. Joy might, for example, ask her students to speculate about the way of life of the Maasai tribes 20 years from now, to hypothesize about a 12-year-old warrior's reaction should he spend a day in their classroom, or to anticipate what might happen if the country of Kenya passed a law against the drinking of animal blood. She could also ask students to consider what they might ask during an interview with a Maasai teenager about his or her way of life.

E-level questions can potentially help middle-level students evaluate tolerantly and ethically: Joy's questions included some of the following:

* What are the advantages and disadvantages of the lifestyle of the Maasai people?
* Should the Maasai tribes be allowed to continue traditional customs, even with a health risk to the members?

- What could the American society learn from the Maasai?
- What would our society have to offer these nomadic peoples?
- What do you admire about the Maasai?
- What do you think you would gain if you spent a few days in a Maasai village?

These E-level questions were constructed to help Joy's sixth graders examine personal and preconceived assumptions that may have been based on limited information, prejudice, or narrow perceptions. Their young adolescent minds are challenged to consider and appreciate culturally different people, to distinguish among the variables that affect lifestyles different from their own, and, one hopes, to develop a broader, less judgmental perspective.

Why the Next Question Matters

The levels in the "Safe" model are designed to elicit from young adolescent students increasingly more complex thinking. The levels are not arranged in a hierarchy of importance, however, because each level can be useful when teachers make decisions about the cognitive needs of individual students. Brophy (1986) suggested that the unit of analysis for effective questioning strategies be shifted from individual question to question sequence. His rationale for sequencing strategies supports the manner in which young adolescents think and learn:

> Sequences beginning with a higher-level question and then proceeding through several lower level follow-up questions would be appropriate for some purposes (asking students to suggest an application of an idea, then probing for details). A different purpose (stimulating students to integrate facts and draw conclusions from them) would require a series of lower-level questions (to recall attention to the relevant facts) followed by higher level questions. (p. 1071)

One purpose for question sequencing is to help young adolescents create meaning out of new information. For example, a teacher might ask, "Do you think Jack is a bad person for going up the beanstalk a third time?" This question might be difficult for a student to answer without consideration of Jack's changing motivation for successive climbs to the giant's quarters. Lower-level questions about Jack's reasons for each climb might serve as information "building blocks" as students attempt to understand the context for Jack's developing greed. The teacher then might re-ask the original E-level question about the third trip and Jack's integrity. Young adolescents, accustomed to the security of literal-response questions, may become frustrated unless teachers sequence questions, thus setting the knowledge base for more challenging levels of thinking.

Wilen and Clegg (1986) observed that students may become anxious when they are unsure of the kind of mental activity required to answer a question. Students, however, can be taught to recognize in questions specific words that "clue" the level of thinking process expected (Strother, 1989). One way for young adolescent students to become more familiar with the question terminology is for them to create their own questions for classroom use. The eighth-grade teacher in the Vonnegut (1968) illustration frequently incorporated student-constructed questions into discussion. Students were aware of the cognitive levels of the "Safe" model, and their questions used the indicative wording. The following questions or question statements were seen scribbled in discernible "middle-school cursive" one day on the chalk board:

- Why do the suitors take so long to realize that Penelope (Homer, 1946) is unweaving the tapestry night after night?
- Speculate what might have happened if Odysseus had returned to find that Penelope had declared him legally dead and remarried.

As sequel to this latter F-level question, the teacher might advance student thinking to the E-level by asking that they appraise the hypothesized situation from Penelope's point of view. For example, if Odysseus had shown anger, would it be justifiable? In this way, teachers can help young adolescents become aware of how their own thinking can progress toward higher cognitive levels.

The earlier application of the "Safe" model in Joy's questioning about the Maasai of Kenya can also illustrate how a teacher might anticipate young adolescent progression of thinking. The following social studies scenario suggests how questions might be sequenced purposefully to build on and extend student thinking:

─────────────────

Safe Scenario 4.1
Social Studies

Possible Questioning Sequence 1

* Describe the physical features of the Rift Valley plateaus where the Maasai settled. (S)
* What is meant by the "steppes of the Maasai"? (S)
* Why have the Maasai remained isolated from the more advanced cultures of western Africa? (A)
* How have the Maasai been able to preserve their many ancient traditions? (A)
* Speculate about Maasai life in Kenya 20 years from now. (F)

Possible Questioning Sequence 2

* What are some of the unique customs of the Maasai? (S)
* Why do the they paint their bodies and decorate their bodies with beads and other ornamentation? (A)
* What can you deduce about their perception of what is beautiful? (A)
* Compare the Maasai hair-cutting ceremonies with American hair salons or barber shops. (A)
* Does style matter to the Maasai? (A)
* Are there other Maasai customs that are similar to any in our society? (A)
* How might a young warrior's react if he spent a day in our classroom? (F)
* What might he say about our fads? (F)

Possible Questioning Sequence 3

* What is the significance of the color red? (A)
* What might happen if the country of Kenya passed a law against the drinking of animal blood? (F)

- Should the Maasai tribes be allowed to continue traditional customs, even with a health risk to the members? (E)

Possible Questioning Sequence 4

- How do the Maasai regard children? cows? other animals? the elderly? (S)
- Are present-day Maasai a warring or peaceful people? (S)
- How do the Maasai govern themselves? (S)
- Why do they place such high value on age groups? (A)
- Would you consider the Maasai a civilized group of people? (E)
- What could the American society learn from the Maasai? (E)
- What would our society have to offer these nomadic peoples? (E)
- What do you admire about the Maasai? (E)

Possible Questioning Sequence 5

- If you could interview a Maasai teenager, what would you ask about his or her way of life? (F)
- What would be some advantages and disadvantages about the lifestyle of the Maasai people? (E)
- What do you think you would gain if you spent time in a Maasai village? (E)

Teachers of young adolescents can use the "Safe" model in other content areas to enhance these students' critical thinking abilities. In an inquiry-based science lab, for example, the teacher might ask students to observe small particles of debris drifting in a water-filled glass container, to recall previous learning about heat and molecular movement, to describe any changes as they gradually heat the water, and to give examples from personal experiences in which heat caused changes in the molecular activity of water. These S-level questions generate personal response and connect with prior experiences.

Students might be asked also to consider the effect of the heating, should the particles be live organisms, or to draw similarities in the observed process to the natural heating of pond or creek water by the sun. They might also be asked to infer the effect of water overheating on plant and animal life or to compare and contrast the effect of an "unnatural" heating of water resources, such as thermal pollution from factories. These are A-level questions that require students to think more analytically about information.

F-level questions could be asked to help students speculate the impact on the environment and community life, should thermal pollution go unregulated. They could be asked to predict the viewpoints of various community members, should a town forum be held. In addition, students might be asked to extend the lab discussion to other real-world examples in which environmental pollution has been regulated by outside agencies.

E-level questions could be posed to guide students into a discussion of the ethics of environmental regulations as infringement on human rights. They would be led to consider the issues of environmental conservation and personal responsibility within a competitive society. Possible ways in which questions might be sequenced are suggested in the following science scenario:

Safe Scenario 4.2
Science

Possible Questioning Sequence 1

* What are the consequences of thermal pollution on plant and fish life in area water bodies? (A)
* What might happen to the environment and community life should thermal pollution become widespread? (F)
* What people would be involved in the issue? (S)
* Should factories assume the expense of relocating waste? (E)

Possible Questioning Sequence 2

* If a town forum were held to debate the issue of factory regulation, what do you think the factory owners might say? the environmentalists? the citizens? the students? (F)
* How might the issue be resolved so that all parties are satisfied? (E)

Possible Questioning Sequence 3

- Name some examples of external regulation of environmental pollution. (S)
- Do you feel the government has the right to restrict industry operations? (E)
- Do these actions infringe on the right to free and competitive enterprise? (E)
- When should environmental concerns override individual rights? (E)

Mathematics is an area where "Safe" questions can be helpful in assisting the young adolescent learner develop skills of reasoning and understanding of complex concepts. Problem-based mathematics puts students into a real-world context and enables them to explore ideas, experiment with and reflect on ideas. These "authentic" problems also motivate young adolescents because they require "real" thinking and understanding beyond the rote memorization of a more traditional approach (Alper, Fendel, Fraser, & Resek, 1996). Working in collaborative groups, young adolescents can examine the problem, pose questions, look for connections, and apply appropriate mathematical skills. Given experience with this inquiry-based approach, students will begin to recognize problem-solving techniques, generalize them to other problem situations, and progressively sharpen them. The next scenario shows a sample mathematical problem followed by suggested questioning sequences. These sequences illustrate possible thought progression as young adolescents work through some problem-solving strategies and later, as they reflect on the process.

Safe Scenario 4.3
Mathematics

A community teen council is concerned about the fat consumption of young adolescents who frequent local fast food establishments. You have been asked to gather data on a typical seventh-grader meal at five of the most popular restaurants in the area. On the basis of this analysis, you are asked to prepare a report to the council advisory board.

Possible Sequence for Preliminary Questions
- What does the task problem ask us to do? (S)
- What information is provided for us in the problem? (S)
- What other information is needed and how can it be found? (A)
- To find out area seventh graders' favorite eating places, what would we need to do? (F)
- How many students must we poll to get a representative sample? (S)
- How can we determine a typical meal? (A)
- Can pizza be reasonably compared to hamburgers? (A)
- What data must be collected to make a comparative analyses? (A)
- What do we do if restaurant owners can't or won't supply what is needed? (F)
- What mathematical calculations will be needed to compare the data? (A)
- What data management program should we use? (A)
- What graphs would best reflect this particular data analysis? (E)
- What information would be most effective to use in the council report? (E)
- How can we best use the talents of the group members? (E)
- What will happen if someone does not follow through with an assignment? (F)
- What other questions do we need to ask? (A)

Possible Sequence for Follow-up Questions
- What problem-solving skills were used to complete the task? (A)
- What barriers were encountered? How could these have been avoided? (A)

- Did the group work cooperatively and effectively? (E)
- What was the strongest point of the group's interaction? (E)
- What specifically would have happened had one member not cooperated? (F)

The young adolescents in the above scenario have applied thinking skills and mathematical concepts to relevant, action-oriented problems. Instead of working through isolated math problems, they practiced the mathematical skills they knew in a meaningful context. They used interpersonal skills and assumed responsibility for delegated work. They made connections with real information, analyzed, synthesized, and presented it in a realistic manner, and learned something about the nutritional habits and preferences of seventh graders. They also better internalized problem-solving skills pertinent to their own cognitive development and growth. They incorporated technology. They also enjoyed learning.

One additional illustration that uses an outdoor problem-solving situation during physical education class shows that the "Safe" model can be used in the nontraditional setting. A group of Ryan's ninth graders might be given the task of passing all members bodily through the open spaces of a human-sized rope "spider web" without touching any of its area or using the same open space more than once. The following "Safe" question sequences, used by both instructor and students, could be helpful in accomplishing this socially, physically and cognitively challenging feat:

Safe Scenario 4.4
Physical Education

Possible Questioning Sequence 1

- What do you view as the most challenging part of the task? (A)
- What other class problem-solving tasks does this one bring to mind? (S)
- What were some specific considerations you had to make before you began the previous task? What were some of

the things that went wrong? What did you learn through your mistakes? (S)

- What must you contribute personally to the challenge? (E)

Possible Questioning Sequence 2

- What might be the advantages of a trial-and-error run? (F)
- What could be the disadvantages of careless errors and unsuccessful attempts? (F)

Possible Questioning Sequence 3

- Why must you choose the spaces carefully for each person? (A)
- How do the spaces compare to the number and size of group members? (S)
- Why is it necessary to think about the size of the first and last persons? (A)
- What might happen if everyone gets through and the last person can't fit through the remaining space? or if the space is out of reach? (F)

These additional evaluative-level questions might be used most effectively to "process" after the task's completion:

- What have you learned about group dynamics that affected or confirmed your understanding of human nature?
- What criteria contributed to successful completion of the task? the unsuccessful attempts?
- What seemed to be your strength in the collaboration process?
- In what areas do you personally need to improve?

The young adolescents in this scenario were guided by the problem-solving questions and encouraged to self-evaluate and group evaluate. Metacognitive skills were practiced as they related previous, more familiar experiences to the present task. They were also encouraged by Ryan to think ahead and to experiment carefully.

Whether the spider web "mission" was ultimately successful was not the main point of the exercise; that students became more aware of how to approach such a task and how to collaborate strategically, however, was. Critical thinking practice in the "safe" setting of even an outdoors classroom should help young adolescents learn effective problem-solving skills to use with other tasks and real-life situations (McBride, 1992).

Linking Student Thinking With Student Learning

The challenge for teachers of young adolescents is to use questioning to help students build new and complex learning structures as they experiment "safely" with a developing capacity for more abstract thought. The cognitive sequencing of questions can help students relate to new knowledge and to think about it in different and more complex ways. Other cognitive processing strategies can help teachers maintain a high level of thinking during class discussions: These techniques also help students achieve much richer learning connections.

One such strategy is the seemingly simple concept of wait time. Wait time is either the pause after a teacher asks a question or the pause after a student gives a response (Rowe, 1986; Tobin, 1987). Rowe (1971) concluded that an average wait time of at least 2.7 seconds improved the length of students' responses and their frequency; this brief pause has also been linked to more logical and speculative thinking, an increase in number of student-initiated questions, more dialogue among students, and an overall boost in student confidence.

A 3-second count might seem a long pause period during class discussion; however, a situation observed in an eighth-grade language arts classroom confirms the young adolescent's need for "think" time. A male student in the back of the room, who had sat silently through most of the class discussion, was asked an analysis-level question by the teacher. Precisely at the count of 3 seconds, the young man voiced a response. Unfortunately, the answer went unheard by the teacher who had simultaneously voiced another student's name across the room to respond to the same question. The original teen gestured in a frustrated manner and slouched down in his desk. The teacher did not call on him again during the remainder of the discussion nor did he initiate any involvement.

Common sense dictates that wait time should vary with the complexity or cognitive level of a question. A factual question may be answered quickly and the teacher can move on to the next question; a higher-level question, however, may require as much as 8 to 10 seconds for students to process information and formulate an appropriate response (Good & Brophy, 1990).

A teacher's pause following a student response has been shown to affect response elaboration. Tobin (1987) explained that if a teacher would refrain from speaking for 3 to 5 seconds after a student's response, the student would sense the expectation to explain further. This postresponse wait time also provides a space of time for other students to add ideas or ask questions. Dillon (1982) projected that if teachers were to avoid speaking at the instant students ended responses, "they would likely hear further expression of higher thought" (p. 141).

Teachers' questioning skills also improve with postresponse wait time. They tend to listen more attentively, to think about students' responses, and to use them as basis for follow-up questions. Teachers' questions tend to be fewer in number, are more purposefully formulated, and elicit higher levels of thinking when teachers pause after students respond (Tobin, 1987).

As discussed in the previous section, what a teacher asks next is important. Deciding what follow-up questions are most "cognitively appropriate," however, is a challenge to most teachers of young adolescents. Follow-up questions can help students give more extensive responses, to clarify or strengthen the logic of their thinking by offering reasons, to substantiate thinking by providing details or examples, and to reflect on their own thinking. This last point contributes to the development of these students' metacognitive abilities at a time when they are becoming increasingly aware of their own problem-solving capacities.

If teachers propose to help young adolescents refine their thinking abilities, they need to put some thought into follow-up questions. Some sample questions that would require young adolescents to think more deeply and sustain a high level of inquiry during a class discussion, include the following:

- What do you mean by . . . ?
- How did you arrive at your response?
- What clues in the story led you to think in that way?
- Why do you think that is a workable solution?
- What ideas did you consider in forming your conclusion?
- Is there anything you could add to your answer?
- Are there other ways of looking at the situation?
- Is there anything else that could be done to solve the problem?
- What makes your idea workable?
- What might be the consequences of your idea? the benefits?
- What would happen if we combined your idea with _____'s idea?

Young adolescent students who seem puzzled about what they have read, who give incorrect responses, who need assistance to respond, or who appear reluctant to participate can benefit from additional cognitive processing strategies. A fifth-grade student, for example, admitted that she was unsure of her position on an issue and asked that she hear other students' ideas before answering. The teacher obliged. A few minutes later the student voluntarily gave her perspective. Later in the discussion, another student responded to an A-level question with "I don't know." The teacher asked the student to read a specific paragraph aloud and look for possible clues to the answer.

Noticing the confusion on a male student's face, the teacher asked if the 10-year-old understood the question. When she rephrased the question, the student was able to respond successfully. Less vocal students can be involved through a follow-up question such as, "Do you agree with that last explanation?" For students who appeared to be responding impulsively, the teacher might ask them to find a passage in the text in which supporting clues are found. For students who tend to stray from the topic with personal stories, reminders can be matter-of-factly given to focus on the current selection. For a reluctant nonvolunteer, the teacher might ask to summarize other perspectives presented thus far in the discussion. Each of these strategies is helpful, nonthreatening, and supportive of the Safe for Thinking philosophy.

Cognitive process techniques help young adolescent students think and make meaningful connections with new learning. These strategies also challenge them to express thinking in a more elaborative and complex manner. Young adolescents will realize that teachers expect responses that reflect good thinking effort and begin to answer less impulsively. Teachers who understand Safe for Thinking strategies ask questions purposefully that help students arrive at deeper levels of understanding and learning. They also make decisions about wait time and question sequencing. In these classrooms, young adolescents feel encouraged to express their thinking because they know it will be accepted and assisted. These "safe" classrooms are inquiry-oriented communities in which teachers and students participate actively and collaboratively as thinkers and learners. An example of the interplay of cognitive and process questions during a class discussion is provided later in the chapter in the "Safe" Scenario 4.5.

Seminars in Session

The following seminar guidelines were written by a group of seventh- and eighth-grade teachers involved in a recent research on teacher questioning and young adolescent cognitive development (Beamon, 1990):

- Give a signal that you want to participate.
- You have the freedom and privilege to disagree with another person's opinion if you provide evidence to support your own viewpoint.
- Each person's ideas are to be respected and valued.
- Each student is expected to be an active participant and an active listener.

The teachers reasoned that young adolescents need structure within which to converse, an open atmosphere within which to interact, and an expectation to be respectful, tolerant, thoughtfully involved, and accountable. These "ground rules" reflect the philosophy of inquiry-based Socratic questioning, which emphasizes participation, nonargumentative debate, tolerant listening, preparation, substantiation of ideas, and focused inquiry.

As seminar leaders, teachers can model the behaviors they expect from young adolescent students. If tolerance among students is expected, for example, teachers can be open to questions and issues that arise; if active listening is expected, teachers can demonstrate this skill by paraphrasing and building on students' responses with follow-up questioning. If teachers want students to entertain alternate viewpoints, they can ask questions that allow for a range of logical responses. If they want students to ask questions, they can raise issues that stimulate inquiry. If they want students to be aware that issues have varying perspectives, they can not insist on common consensus. If they want students to reexamine assumptions based on new evidence, they can model open-mindedness.

Similarly, if teachers of young adolescents want students to respond thoughtfully to questions, they must be sure students understand the level of thinking anticipated. If they want students to engage in more complex thinking, they must pose follow-up questions that delve and challenge. If they want students to become independent thinkers, they must make them conscious of their own thinking processes. If they want these young adolescents to become better thinkers, they must provide encouragement, practice, and challenge. For a humorous pause, the reader might enjoy the author's top ten list of things NOT to do during seminar discussion.

TOP TEN List on
"How to Fail at Leading
a Stimulating Discussion"

10. Only ask questions that you know how to answer.

9. Call on only those students who raise their hands.

8. Insist on common agreement.

7. Don't expect students to support or explain answers.

6. Don't embarrass student by waiting for responses.

5. Encourage argument.

4. Discourage students from asking questions.

3. Be determined to ask all the questions on your list.

2. Ask mostly lower-level questions.

1. Remember, a little humiliation only fortifies the spirit.

The following classroom seminar illustrates inquiry-based questioning techniques and the kind of interaction patterns that support and motivate young adolescent thinking development.

Inquiry and Interaction
in the Middle-Level Classroom

Kali's sixth-grade students were accustomed to seminar discussion. Kali had been involved in local staff development sponsored by the nearby Paideia Institute the previous summer. Students were familiar with seminar "ground rules." They also understood the expectation to come to class prepared with at least three questions about the previous night's reading, Shirley Jackson's (1951) short story *Charles*. That meant reading it—carefully. The students also knew how to formulate thought-provoking questions "worthy" of discussion time. Seminar discussion was perceived as fun by Kali's students because they did most of the talking, and everyone had a chance to speak. If they could not remember something, they were encouraged to check back in the story. In fact, Kali often directed them to check certain passages for clues to answers. No one was allowed to laugh at a wrong answer; the stories they read were always interesting, many with mysterious happenings and surprise endings; and the period always passed quickly.

Kali instructed students to "put on their thinking caps" and opened the seminar with the question, "Why did Laurie invent Charles?" Jimmy quickly signaled and responded, "To cover up for the bad things he was doing in school." Kali smiled, paused a few seconds and called on Lucy, whose hand had shot up soon after Jimmy's. "To get attention," came her answer. Kali then redirected the question by saying, "Does anyone have another idea why Laurie invented Charles?"

Noticing a look of confusion on Jerry's face, Kali asked, "Do you think there is a boy in kindergarten named Charles?" When Jerry said he had thought so, Kali asked him to reread the last sentence of the story. As it turned out, Jerry had neglected to look on the back page of his copy of the story. "Oh," he exclaimed, "it was Laurie doing all those bad things, not Charles." "Is that why you think he invented Charles?" asked Kali, to which Jerry responded, "Yes, I agree with Jimmy."

Kali reiterated the responses thus far, and asked if there were other ideas. Thoughtfully, Mary volunteered a different response, "Actually, I think he was having adjustment problems with kindergarten." Kali probed, "Can you explain how you reasoned that Laurie might be having an adjustment problem in kindergarten?" "Well, he acted out at home by talking disrespectfully to his father. At school, he acted out by throwing the chalk, hitting the teacher, and saying a cuss word to that little girl," Mary richly elaborated.

Before Kali could speak again, Pete signaled from across the room with the question, "If Laurie was acting out so bad in school, why didn't the teacher call home?" Helen quickly suggested, "Maybe he wasn't really doing all those bad things. Maybe he made some of them up to get attention." "Do you agree with Lucy that Laurie invented Charles to get attention?" posed Kali. "Yes," came the reply from Helen.

"Would you consider Laurie a behavioral problem?" Kali opened a related line of questioning. Responses varied, each with firm rationale. "Does Laurie remind you of anyone you know?" ventured Kali. "He reminds me of my little brother," exclaimed one student. "He reminds me of Dennis the Menace!" another blurted, "always trying to get Mr. Wilson's attention." Tim jumped in with, "I bet he was jealous of the new baby." "Do you think Laurie is trying to put on a new identity?" offered Kali, to which Tim said, "I'm not sure." "Read the first paragraph of the story aloud for us and see if we can find any clues." "Well," Tim tried again after reading the section aloud, "maybe he was tired of wearing bibbed overalls . . . and he didn't even wave to his mom at the corner." "Would you consider him a behavioral problem?" re-asked Kali.

The questioning continued in the same fashion, sequenced to elicit different levels of thinking and more thoughtful levels of consideration. When a student asked why the father didn't go the P.T.A. meeting, Kali filled in a little background about the period in which Jackson had written the story. Seizing an opportunity, Kali asked, "What might have happened if the father had gone to the first meeting?" (which the mother missed because the baby was sick). Later, he asked, what might have happened if the mother had not gone to the second P.T.A. meeting?

Many students struggled with one of Kali's questions, "Why did Laurie have a relapse just before the second P.T.A. meeting?" "What do you think a relapse means?" offered the teacher. Mary responded immediately, "A setback. It means he was good and then acted bad again." Kali followed up with another lower-level question, asking students to find evidence in the story to show Laurie's "relapse" or "setback."

When Kali re-asked, "Why did Laurie have a relapse just prior to the second P.T.A. meeting?," students were able to make connections among the attention-seeking factor, the adjustment problem, and the mother's impending visit to the second kindergarten meeting. Kali posed again, "Would you consider Laurie a behavioral problem?" Student responses at this point began to reflect a better understanding of Laurie's possible motivations, and the discussion seemed less critical of the young kindergartner's actions. Then Kali threw out a ringer, "How would the story have changed had there really been a Charles!?"

The following "Safe" scenario provides examples for additional questioning sequences that include follow-up process questions for the story *Charles*. Sequence 3 illustrates the use of lower-level questions to enable students to construct textual information to respond meaningfully to the more difficult higher-level question that began the sequence. The process questions are denoted by an asterisk (*).

Safe Scenario 4.5
Language Arts

Possible Questioning Sequence 1

- Is there a boy in kindergarten named Charles? (S)
- *How do you know that Laurie made up Charles? (elaboration, substantiation)
- How would you compare Laurie's behavior at home with Charles behavior at school? (A)
- Why does Laurie invent Charles? (A)
- *What clues in the story make you think that? (textual support)
- *Is there another reason why Laurie might have invented Charles? (extension and redirection of A-level question)

Possible Questioning Sequence 2

- Do you think Laurie's teacher should have called his parents? (E)
- Do you think Laurie did all the things he described about Charles? (A)
- Name some of the "bad" things Charles did at school? (S)
- How would you compare Laurie's behavior at home with Charles's behavior at school? (A)
- Do you know someone about Laurie's age? (S)
- Would you consider Laurie a behavioral problem? (E)

Possible Questioning Sequence 3

- Why do you think Laurie had a relapse just before the P.T.A. meeting? (A)
- Was Laurie having trouble adjusting to kindergarten? (S)
- *How do you know? (support)
- Is there a time when he seems to have adjusted? (S)
- *What indicates that to you? (probing, support)
- Why do you think he became the teacher's helper in the third week? (A)
- Why would he have a relapse just before the P.T.A. meeting? (shift to original higher A-level question)

Possible Questioning Sequence 4

- Why do you think Laurie's parents are more interested in Charles's behavior than the behavior of their own son? (A)
- Why don't Laurie's parents guess that Charles doesn't exist? (A)
- How might the story have changed had Laurie's mother gone to the first P.T.A. meeting? (F)
- What might have happened had Laurie's mother not gone to the second meeting? (F)
- *Describe your thinking for that response. (probing, metacognition)
- *Is there something else that might have happened? (extension)

- What do you think Laurie's mother says to Laurie when she arrives home? (F)
- Do you think Laurie should be punished? (E)
- *Explain your response. (probing, substantiation)

Summary

A humorist once noted that it is better to know some of the questions than all of the answers. Inquiry-based instruction, whether used in language arts class, social studies, science, math, or the nontraditional setting of the gymnasium or outdoor trail, can be a powerful teacher tool for stimulating young adolescent thinking. Cognitive research has expanded teachers' understanding of the instructional power of question sequencing. The "Safe" model offers teachers of young adolescents a scheme for constructing questions on four cognitive levels; skillful sequencing of questions can help students make meaningful connections with new knowledge and to think more deeply about new learning. The research has also altered the traditional role of the teacher from disseminator of information to fellow inquirer. The following additional application of the SAFE acronym (Beamon, 1990) serves as summary:

- Sequencing of questions
- Attitudes of teacher and students
- Follow-up techniques
- Emphasis on cognitive processing

Teacher and student interaction during inquiry-based instruction reflects true communication: All participants listen, consider, and contribute. Collaboration, cooperation, and response opportunity are evident as social behaviors reflect a respect for the thinking-in-action. The teacher's questions guide and challenge but do not lead or predetermine students' responses. Teachers of students in this developmental age group are challenged to negotiate the terrain between student understanding and deeper levels of thinking and learning. The cognitive processing strategies of postquestion and postresponse wait time; follow-up questions that probe for explanation, elaboration, substantiation, or metacognition; and the integration of student questioning can help teachers meet this challenge. The dynamics created through such inquiry-based interaction are rich for young adolescent thinking development.

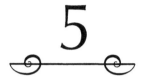

5

Assessing Through Products and Performance

If a nation could be tested into excellence, America would be the smartest country in the world.

Jonathan Kozol (1994)

Timmy: I taught my cat Domino how to tap dance.
Joey: I don't see her dancing.
Timmy: I said I taught her. I didn't say she learned it.

Glenda Ward Beamon

Overview

When Carolyn wanted to find out what her seventh graders had learned during their study of Egyptian culture, she could have designed the traditional unit test, with fill-in-the-blank questions, matching items, and a "killer" essay question. Instead, she chose to pose the following situation for response:

You have been asked to talk to an international committee formed to decide the fate of the newly discovered tomb of a famous pharaoh in the Valley of the Kings. Excavation and restoration would allow the tomb to be opened to the public, a boost to Egypt's important tourist industry. Funds are lacking, however, in Egypt's struggling economy, to bring in the technology necessary to preserve yet another monument. Write a persuasive speech that addresses why the restoration would be important historically and economically to the Egyptians, and how international support could help to protect the ancient site from pollution and neglect.

To respond to this scenario, students would need to be knowledgeable of the ancient Egyptian reverence for cultural antiquity (and why) and of current-day problems inherent in excavation, conservation, and economic progress. Naturally, Carolyn's students had numerous opportunities to read about and discuss Egypt's fascinating history and its modern-day challenges.

Carolyn's method of testing reflects the current trend in the assessment of student thinking and learning, a new approach that involves students more meaningfully in the assessment experience. Wiggins (1993) used the term *authentic* to describe alternative assessment that demonstrates students' understanding and learning through products, performance, problem solving, or exhibition. Gardner (1993) similarly proposed that a "good" assessment instrument be the learning experience itself. Alternative, nontraditional measures are developmentally appropriate for young adolescents because they provide valuable information to teachers about student thinking and learning progress. Goals can be set and improvement recognized. Assessment that focuses on the thinking and learning process represents a more accurate, positive, and motivational method of following the thinking development and ongoing learning of young adolescents.

Chapter 5 describes meaningful assessment within the Safe for Thinking classroom environment. The purpose of the chapter is to offer teachers a repertoire of assessment options that provide a truer picture of young adolescent thinking and learning progress. Guidelines are given for the evaluation of a variety of student learning performances, problem solving, and collaborative group tasks. A method of analysis for classroom thinking interaction during group discussion is provided as well as a way to determine when students' oral responses to questions indicate higher levels of thinking expression. The chapter culminates with a closer look at meaningful assessment in Carolyn's seventh-grade social studies classroom.

What's New in Assessment for Young Adolescents and Why

Contrary to traditional belief, young adolescent learning does not always have to be graded, nor is it evaluated best through paper-and-pencil tests. Lazear (1994) wrote of a new assessment paradigm that respects individual and varied differences among students, that focuses on ongoing development and improvement, and that connects with and, ideally, helps prepare students for living and learning beyond the classroom. Wiggins (1993) has argued that educators today need to place less emphasis on obtaining precise scores and more on the "intellectual value of the challenge" (p. 202). Gardner (1991) has described student understanding as the capacity to apply what has been learned to new situations. Intellectual challenge, real-world situations, application of knowledge, multiple learning experiences, and individual student progress are what meaningful assessment is about.

In his book, *The Unschooled Mind*, Gardner (1991) contended that assessment in education should be an ongoing effort to distinguish among various levels of student learning performance. When one considers young adolescent thinking in terms of a continuing and developmental process, the idea of helping students recognize where they are and where they need to go makes sense. Olympic performers are aware of certain criteria they must meet for a particular score level or ranking. Although perfect "10s" are rare even among the world's best athletes, varying levels of quality are generally recognizable to the evaluative eye. Students similarly can become aware of criteria that distinguish better from poor thinking, and of certain performance criteria that indicate a higher quality of thinking toward which they should strive. Continuous and meaningful assessment enables teachers to help young adolescents to distinguish among levels of thinking quality and to understand how they personally "measure up" to criteria for the highest standard of performance.

Gardner (1991) has used the sports analogy of "benchmarks" for various points or levels along a performance continuum that might run from poor to better to best thinking. Teachers need to help young adolescents understand the criteria that distinguish between and among these progressive levels of performance. The criteria that determine "needs work," in other words, should be differentiated from those that determine "getting better" or "better." For these benchmarks to be meaningful and useful indicators of progress, they need to be well defined, clearly communicated, and mutually understood by teachers and students. Young adolescents, in turn, need to understand what specifically about their personal thinking endeavors places them at one point or another along the continuum. Meaningful evaluative feedback from teachers can help guide students from benchmark to benchmark as they progress toward better thinking practice. If the intent is to foster and guide young adolescent cognitive development, then assessment should purposefully parallel and contribute to students' improvement efforts.

Using the term *benchmark* to describe a student's progress along a continuum toward increasingly higher levels of performance implies that an "end point" might ultimately be attained. Although one can understandably argue against "scoring a perfect 10" on the thinking continuum, it is important that students and teachers understand what constitutes quality performance. In Chapter 2, reference was made to characteristic "habits of mind" or "intellectual standards" for thinking (Ennis, 1987; Paul, 1994, 1996). These standards represent a teacher's highest expectations for student thinking. These expectations can be placed on young adolescents' verbal communication and other learning and thinking avenues such as problem solving, project development, and written products. Young adolescents need to understand the indicators for "best thinking performance" to concentrate their best efforts. Just as young adolescents need to recognize how they currently "measure up," they need to have a good idea of where they should be headed.

A teacher, for example, might have certain expectations for the quality of student responses during class discussion. These might include clarity of expression, specificity, logic, accuracy, or depth (Paul, 1996). The teacher would need to define and communicate these expectations as elements of "good" thinking expression and as standards for thinking toward which the students should progress. Clarity might be defined as the ability to give examples or illustrations, to restate, rephrase, paraphrase, or condense. The teacher could explain and model examples of good reasoning aloud in front of the class. The teacher's informal assessment of the quality of the students' verbal communication, however, will likely reveal the need for a bit of guidance! In other words, the teacher will need to help students move along the "quality continuum" from responses that indicate faulty or poor reasoning or a lack of clarity or depth to those that reflect better thought processing. Young adolescents need to know where they are and where they should be headed; they also need assistance in getting there.

One way in which teachers can guide students toward increasingly better thinking "habits" is through process questioning, as described in Chapter 4. If teachers apply the standard of clarity to students' thinking expression, for example, they may ask such questions as, Explain what you mean? Express your ideas in another way? Give an example of what you are trying to say? If teachers want to encourage more depth or insightful thinking in verbal expression, they might ask students to give a more complex explanation or to look for a relationship between what they are saying and another student's explanation. If teachers want students to pay attention to the skills of logic, they might ask, How does that follow what you just said? or How do these relate? For specificity, teachers can ask for detail; for accuracy, teachers can ask for proof or evidence. In each of these examples, teachers are "pushing" for a certain quality, level, or depth of thinking expression. Ultimately, the goal is for students to internalize these "standards" so they can evaluate their own thinking processes and progress (Paul, 1996).

In the following example, a seventh-grade teacher uses process questioning to try to elicit responses based on more complex student thinking about an incident in Shirley Jackson's (1951) short story *Charles*.

> *Teacher:* Why do you think Laurie had a relapse just before the second P.T.A. meeting?
>
> *Janie:* Cause he might have had some friends in kindergarten and wanted to show off for them. (vague, general response)

Teacher: Could you elaborate on what you mean? (pushes for clarity)

Janie: Well, he had probably made a lot of friends when he started being a good boy, helping the teacher and being nice. Maybe he just wanted to act out again and show off. (draws in some support for answer; attempts some reasoning)

Teacher: Do you see any connection between Laurie's relapse and the fact that his mother was coming to the P.T.A. meeting? (pushes for depth)

Janie: Possibly . . . maybe he thought the teacher would ask the mother about the attitude change and then she'd know there was no "Charles." (makes a connection in story events)

Teacher: Why do you think he had a relapse just before the P.T.A. meeting? (repeats original question)

Janie: I wonder if Laurie really wanted his mother to make the connection. Maybe he wanted her to realize about his adjustment problems at last. (attempts at some insight into character motivation)

As the teacher guides Janie toward clearer, more elaborative, and better substantiated response, he or she challenges this young adolescent to think with more depth about the situation in the story. The teacher's probing questions communicate an expected standard for verbal response, and the student is consequently held accountable for what is articulated and the quality of the thinking behind it.

Student debate is another area that can serve as an example of this interplay of "end point" standards, progressive "benchmarks," and meaningful assessment. Suppose Carolyn's problem situation at the beginning of this chapter had been structured in the form of a debate (based on information from Franquet & Sattin, 1996). The task might read as follows:

The tomb of a famous pharaoh has been discovered in the Valley of the Kings. Its excavation, restoration, and maintenance would drain the financial resources of Egypt's struggling economy; yet its boost to Egypt's tourism could be significant. Choose one side and prepare for a debate over the fate of this newly found cultural treasure.

To get ready for the anticipated debate, young adolescents would need to research various and current perspectives on the issue of how best to preserve Egyptian antiquity. They would need to determine and analyze the assumptions on which various perspectives are based, such as the foreign archaeologist who is interested in personal glory or the local preservationist concerned with the protection of historical relics. Students would need to formulate and respond to the question of whether the financial risk of restoration and maintenance would outweigh the potential economic benefit. In addition, they would need to consider the consequences of certain decisions about the fate of the tomb. Each of these considerations plays into the quality of the position the students ultimately take on the issue.

To assess the quality of the students' reasoning during the debate, the teacher and students might consider the following questions: How clearly did specific students state their positions? How logically and consistently did the students defend their position? How fair were the students in regard to alternate perspectives? To what extent did the students deal with the complexity of the issue or questions explored (Paul & Elder, 1994)? Young adolescents need to become aware of the expectations for quality reasoning that are reflected in their verbal expression. They also need evaluative feedback as to how they are progressing, and they need help in recognizing the indicators of thinking progress and improvement.

When young adolescents consistently hear questions such as in the previous examples, they can begin to internalize them as questions they need to ask themselves, even without prompting or feedback from the teacher. Paul (1996) refers to an inner voice that students develop that guides, monitors, and improves their personal thinking and reasoning processes. Young adolescent learners are rapidly developing the cognitive skills that enable them to think about their own thinking, and they can begin to discern differences in its quality. With expectation and guidance, they will attempt to be more clear or more precise in their verbal expression, for example, or take the time to reason instead of impulsively blurting out a response. They will more naturally look for underlying meaning and connections in related information. They should more readily consider the alternative perspective as they weigh the sides of an issue. Young adolescents can become better thinkers at a period in their lives when thinking capacity is fast developing and when they can be conscious of its actual development and improvement.

A Few More Examples

Ongoing assessment provides teachers with continuous data to monitor students' needs and progress; it guides students as they explore and experiment, and it encourages them to reflect on and evaluate their own progress. The teachers' expected standards for quality become recognizable "thinking goals" toward which young adolescents aspire. Young adolescents' expanding metacognitive skills better equip them to distinguish among the levels of quality in what they say or write or produce or perform. They can begin to notice "benchmarks" of personal progress and strive for continued improvement. Teachers likewise can assess how students are "measuring up" to expectations, provide feedback, and help students continually improve.

The reader might consider an example of assessment and young adolescent social skill development. Although inclined to interact, young adolescents are not necessarily proficient in the ability to work effectively in collaborative groups. Teachers and students need to discuss and establish criteria for productive group behavior, and goals need to be set. The success of the group will depend on individual contribution, participation, cooperation, and collaboration. To evaluate how they and other members are measuring up to group expectations, students need to be cognizant of the indicators for group productivity: Did each member contribute an idea? Did students listen to each other? Were various ideas considered? Was the group able to reach consensus or make a decision or complete a task well? In this example students would have to be aware of the criteria for expected behavior, aware of their own behavior, and aware of the behavior of other members of the group. Assessment would actually begin before the task as expectations are discussed, continue during the collaborative process as students "mentally monitor" the group interaction, and culminate with the follow-up evaluation in which students discuss how they did and what they need to do better.

Group problem solving is an excellent way for meaningful assessment to help young adolescents develop and improve cognitive skills. Groups of students can be given problem tasks similar to the situation at the beginning of the chapter. Following group discussion, the teacher might ask students to identify some of the thinking skills used during the problem-solving process. For example, did they gather data, examine evidence, analyze and test ideas? Did they question the validity of evidence? Did they make assumptions? Did they test these assumptions? Did they develop a plan? Did they break the problem into smaller parts and assign tasks? What kind of thinking did they use to arrive at the problem's solution? The teacher can also provide information from his or her observation during the problem-solving process. This "debriefing" strategy helps young adolescents recognize the personal cognitive processes used during problem solving: They also are using their developing metacognitive capabilities. Additional practice in other simulated tasks or problems can help students generalize, transfer, and thus reinforce problem-solving skills. The ultimate assessment, and one in which teachers can only hope that "inner voice" is speaking clearly, is when young adolescents need to activate these problem-solving skills in real-life situations.

Used formally or informally, daily or summatively, meaningful assessment can be a positive tool for young adolescent cognitive development. Assessment can help teachers check for students' genuine understanding and learning and help young adolescents become more cognitively aware of unfolding thinking capacities. Through class discussion, debate, simulation, multimedia presentation, or other learning experiences, young adolescents can demonstrate their level of understanding, its quality can be determined, and the information applied to subsequent situations. Other examples of meaningful and ongoing assessment-in-action are provided throughout this and the next chapter. Realistic, well-defined "benchmarks" connected progressively to well-established "end points" or standards can motivate, guide, and challenge students to pay attention to the quality of their own thinking—and to improve on it!

The Assessment Dilemma

Alternative assessment represents a new way to measure more meaningfully young adolescent learning and thinking. Performance assessment conveys to students that what is valued is not the mere memorization of isolated bits of information but their ability to apply knowledge and understanding in new situations and through high-quality products (Willis, 1996). The trend reflects movement away from norm-referenced tests, which compare students against each other, to criterion-referenced measures that evaluate students against specified standards and performance levels. For young adolescents, this less traditional form of measuring success actually creates success because students are assessed against a continuum of personal improvement rather than against other students' performance. The challenge to individual students lies in getting better, not in competing with or outperforming classmates.

Alternative assessment offers several advantages to the young adolescent learner. The focus on individual improvement supports the development and expansion of these students' "budding" cognitive skills. When they are actively involved in developing assessment criteria, they tend to recognize what it means to do well and can better monitor personal efforts to do so. Alternative assessment also gives young adolescents an opportunity to express their thinking and learning through multiple avenues—dramatics, music, artistic performance, verbal and written expression—certainly important in this time of experimentation and exploration. In addition, alternative assessment coupled with traditional paper-and-pencil tests paints a truer picture of young adolescents' progress and improvement during a period in their lives when positive development is so critical.

Then what is the dilemma? Why is performance assessment not in widespread use by teachers of young adolescents? One reason is that this alternative form of assessment is more difficult to develop and more time-consuming to administer (Wiggins, 1993). Teachers, in addition, feel pressured to meet systemwide student learning objectives that are most often measured through end-of-grade or end-of-course tests. Unless more latitude is provided teachers for the assessment of student learning and thinking, these constraints will continue to inhibit. Furthermore, it may take a leap of faith for educators to accept the idea that student learning is more effectively measured through a performance-based extension of the actual learning experience. A well-accepted example is student writing assessment. The holistic evaluation of writing has been in use for a number of years; however, the transfer of performance-based criteria to other learning products, such as problem solving or dramatic production, is not as common a practice.

Willis (1996) acknowledged the educational concern that performance-based assessment is less valid, less reliable, and less objective. If the intent is to monitor and improve student thinking, however, validity is reflected in how well the measurement procedure assesses the thinking process. A standardized instrument or a multiple choice test is limited in capturing the dynamics of group problem solving or a student's use of logic during a critical response, whether oral or written. More traditional measurement tends also to be removed from the actual learning experience and may be limited in reflecting students' true understanding of the content studied (Wiggins, 1993).

Reliability is concerned with the extent to which the assessment procedure provides consistent results. With the performance format, student are assessed against a continuum of personal improvement, not against other students' performance. If teachers clearly define and communicate criteria for levels of performance, and if these are understood, the consistency needed to establish reliability is maintained. Also, simple steps such as requesting students to code papers with social security or telephone numbers in lieu of names, permitting peer review and including other teachers in the scoring of major products can help ensure the reliability of performance assessment.

As for objectivity, when desired "thinking outcomes" are known, when progress points are established and recognized, and when students learn to discern the criteria for quality differences, performance assessment provides a better representation of student understanding, learning, and thinking development. Standards for good thinking can furthermore be transferred to other performance tasks and to content domains. For example, young adolescents can use skills of reasoning during class discussion, when writing a persuasive essay, or when conducting a scientific experiment. The ability to make in-depth connections among pieces of information can be assessed through debate, dramatic role play, or musical composition. Young adolescents' expanding metacognitive skills can be assessed through reflective journals and independent research projects. Wiggins (1993) refers to a search for "patterns" of response across a variety of learning experiences as students work for consistency in thinking performance. Also, when students are exposed to real-world and relevant situations, they are more apt to transfer both learning and thinking processes to personal lives.

Other teacher concerns revolve around the question of grading. Letter grades are generally the expectation. Teachers, however, can decide which performance products are significant to warrant a grade and which can be evaluated through rubric scoring only or through specific teacher, peer, or self-comments. In each case, the key is for teachers to develop specific criteria to define quality performance levels. Evaluative criteria should reflect both the thinking anticipated and content knowledge gained. For example, a position letter on whether China's one-child policy is a violation of human rights should reflect a student's ability to organize information into a coherent and properly written letter format. The criteria should also reflect the student's understanding of China's political and economic culture and the cognitive skill to consider both sides of the issue. How to develop scoring rubrics for performance evaluation is discussed in the next section.

Certainly the public needs a bit of convincing, and this point is a significant part of the quandary (Willis, 1996). Parents are accustomed to the language of traditional assessment and grading practices, and they generally want to know how their youngsters are performing in relation to other students in the class. They need to understand what it means for students' progress to be measured relative to performance criteria. One fifth-grade teacher meets this challenge by inviting parents and students to periodic "portfolio showing" nights. Students share written work and other products displayed around the room, explain to parents what the grading criteria are and why, and talk about the progress they have shown over the period of time. An eighth-grade teacher explains what a scoring rubric is by having parents examine samples of student writing at the back-to-school open house. These efforts help parents begin to understand how performance assessment benefits individual students by allowing for improvement within reasonable expectations. Parents may also notice a positive change in their youngsters' motivation level toward learning and school in general!

Of course, the concern goes beyond the young adolescents' parents. The cry for accountability among state legislatures has caused many local school systems to tighten expectations on student performance, and this performance is more commonly, easily, and economically measured through the more traditional testing format. These constraints, as indicated earlier, understandably limit the way teachers of young adolescents teach and measure learning. Some states, however, have developed performance-based tasks to assess student progress (North Carolina Education Standards and Accountability Commission, 1995). Others have begun to provide training in performance assessment, to incorporate real-world, problem-solving, and hands-on tasks into statewide assessment measures, and to sponsor local and regional assessment consortia (see Willis, 1996). In time, perhaps these initiatives and state-mandated accountability will dovetail in recognition of a more enlightened way to measure student learning and thinking development.

When young adolescents understand the criteria against which their learning and thinking are evaluated, when they understand where they stand and where they hope to go to improve, they are more motivated to give their best to the learning situation. Teachers in Safe for Thinking classrooms provide this motivation through meaningful assessment. Examples of the way assessment can tie directly to the curriculum are provided in the following sections and in Chapter 6.

Performance Assessment
and Evaluation

Many researchers in the area of cognitive development suggest that real learning has not taken place unless students can transfer that learning to situations beyond the classroom (Lazear, 1994). Solving realistic problems, debating current issues, simulating real-life situations, writing, publishing, or performing for real-world audiences are examples of instructional strategies that make thinking and learning relevant for young adolescents (Gallagher & Gallagher, 1994). Wiggins (1993) claimed that "the criterion of a good test is its congruence with reality" (p. 206). Carolyn's summative assessment of her students' understanding of Egyptian culture, past and present, is an example.

Carolyn had to come to terms with several factors in her decision against the more traditional assessment format. First, she may have asked herself, For what do I really want students to be accountable and how can I best assess their understanding? (Of course, the answers to these questions also determined how she approached planning and teaching of the unit.) What was important to Carolyn was that her students not only gain knowledge of ancient Egyptian religious beliefs, values, and customs but that they also acquire an understanding of Egypt's current and ongoing environmental and economic concerns. Even more important, she wanted them to try to conceptualize the relationship of a country's past and present culture. To assess this understanding Carolyn designed a performance task that thrust her seventh graders into a realistic and relevant problem situation.

Carolyn could have asked students to respond to an essay question about the problem of preserving Egyptian monuments. She could have asked students to name a recent discovery in the Valley of the Kings or to describe why the Egyptians valued their ancient tombs, or even to explain the importance of tourism to modern Egypt's economy. Any of these questions address important information to know and recall. Instead, she asked students to use what they had learned in each of these areas, and to use their evaluative skills in the context of a persuasive piece of writing. Reread Carolyn's assessment task and consider the level of thinking needed to respond:

You have been asked to talk to an international committee formed to decide the fate of the newly discovered tomb of a famous pharaoh in the Valley of the Kings. Excavation and restoration would allow the tomb to be opened to the public, a boost to Egypt's important tourist industry. Funds are lacking, however, in Egypt's struggling economy, to bring in the technology necessary to preserve yet another monument. Write a persuasive speech that addresses why the restoration would be important historically and economically to the Egyptians and how international support could help protect the ancient site from pollution and neglect.

This task created for the students a simulation about a plausible, real-world situation that would motivate by its relevance and challenge.

Naturally, Carolyn was faced with the challenge of assigning a grade to the students' performance on the task, probably the reason most of her colleagues clung to more traditional assessment measures. Grading meant establishing some criteria for scoring. What would denote an exemplary product from an acceptable or unacceptable one? How would an "A" paper differ from a "B"? In addition, there was the matter of format and resources. How much time could be allowed for the composition? Would students be permitted to use notes or to collaborate? Should students actually deliver the speeches, certainly ensuring authenticity for the task?

Carolyn ultimately decided that students should work individually to write the speeches. She reasoned that an exemplary paper should reflect a strong understanding of the dilemma modern-day

Egypt faces in trying to promote tourism and in preserving its national treasures. She decided on the following criteria for an "A" paper:

An explanation why monument restoration is important to the present-day Egyptians culturally and economically

At least two reasons why funds are needed to preserve the excavated structures

At least two reasons why financial assistance from the international committee was important

A logically developed and well-written argument

Acceptable reasons why funds were needed might include the use of technology for special lighting, structural support, protective barriers against tourists, and natural pollutants. Pertinent reasons to justify financial assistance might include promotion of global relations, benefit to world economy, international investment in a struggling Third World economy, or international pride in cultural antiquity. Students could thus draw from a range of knowledge to develop the best argument.

Carolyn's students found the task exciting, intriguing, and challenging. They had discussed the sacred and artful process of mummification and the time-consuming construction of the ancient pyramids and temples, and they had been fascinated by the Egyptian reverence for the afterlife. They had viewed video footage of hieroglyphics on the walls of the temples, the artists' colors amazingly preserved for thousands of years. (They also knew that visitors to the unprotected tombs in the Valley of the Kings deposited gallons of sweat daily, causing this paint and plaster to peel from the walls.)

The seventh graders had debated the pros and cons of allowing foreign Egyptologists to excavate in the Valley of the Kings—and had been amused by the story of Lord Carnarvon and his death by mosquito. They had talked about the successful campaign fought by UNESCO in the 1960s to move Abu Simbel above the waterline of the new Aswan Dam. Now, Carolyn was giving them the challenge of addressing an international council that could help solve a feasible problem. To respond to the performance task, they would have to use their understanding of the content studied and integrate, synthesize, and apply this understanding within the context of situation described in the question. Challenging, you bet, but beats "multiple guess" questions, as one student commented!

Developmental Assessment
in "Process"

Young adolescence is a time of tremendous growth and change for students, ages 10 to 14. For assessment to be a developmental strategy, it must be both progress and process oriented. Another area in which developmental assessment can be used is student writing. Although the writing process is discussed more fully in Chapter 6, a brief description at this point illustrates ongoing writing assessment. Journals allow young adolescent students to collect and experiment with new ideas, as well as a chance to respond to specific assigned topics. These ideas are owned by the students and not evaluated until or if they are selected for more structured writing tasks. These tasks might include letters to historical characters, editorials about current issues, poetry, short stories, legends, speeches, advertisements—the list goes on and on. Teachers and students can work together to establish the criteria for evaluation based on the particular kind of writing, the specific skills she has taught, and the content. At times, Carolyn uses varying levels of these criteria to fashion a rubric with assigned point values; these values, however, are not necessarily equivalent to letter or numerical grades. A sample rubric for an advertisement to promote Egyptian travel is shown below.

3 = Accurate information about five or more sites of interest
   Effective use of descriptive writing
   Creative format to entice visitors or persuade travel
   Correct editing
2 = Less than five sites or inaccurate information
   Descriptive writing lacks detail
   Needs minor editing
1 = Needs to expand content about sites of interest
   Minimal use of description
   Major editing required for improvement

Students are given the opportunity to edit and improve in most instances, thus allowing them to progress toward better written products.

"Authentic assessment," as defined by Wiggins (1989), involves meaningful tasks at which students can learn to excel. Because the young adolescent is rapidly and continuously developing skills, talents, and abilities, an effort to "track" the pattern of this development seems appropriate. Writing portfolios enable young adolescents to monitor their writing progress throughout the year. These portfolios include student-selected samples of work, peer evaluations, and teacher comments. The portfolios are periodically shared with parents. What the young adolescents begin to recognize over the year is a pattern of progress and improvement in their writing. The students' metacognitive skills develop as they become more aware of the progression of both thinking and writing skills. Of course, the portfolios do not remain limited to student writing. When Carolyn's students began adding video tapes of skits, photographs of projects, and computer diskettes for multimedia presentations they had designed, she asked a local pizza chain to donate the cardboard boxes to more easily contain the growing variety of student work!

Gardner (1991) extends the portfolio assessment approach to the more process-oriented strategy of the "process folio" (p. 240). The "process folio" reveals the various stages in the development of a project, product, or artistic work. It might include early ideas, drafts, work collected during the planning stages, critiques by peers, personal comments, final products, and reflections as to how the entire process might be improved in the future. This assessment method encourages students to collect, reflect on, and evaluate their own progress. The "process folio" strategy also gives teachers an opportunity to assess student understanding more fully and to monitor (and celebrate!) thinking development over a period of time. This assessment is developmentally appropriate for young adolescent cognitive development.

When Thinking Is Observable

If the reader could slip into the back of a classroom in which young adolescents were involved in group discussion, what would be observable about this learning experience that would indicate a thinking climate? What actions would indicate that the teacher was teaching for thinking? What discernible behaviors among the students would indicate that they were engaged in high level thinking activity? Furthermore, what might indicate to the teacher that these young adolescents were not only developing their thinking skills but also improving them through involvement in the inquiry-oriented discussion? This section describes an observation tool designed to follow instructional interaction during classroom discussion and to give an indication of teachers' use of thinking-supportive practices. The subsequent section presents a model through which teachers can analyze students' verbal responses to questions and determine when these responses reflect more refined thinking expression.

The reader might recall the earlier description of the seminar interaction during Kali's sixth graders' discussion of *Charles* (Jackson, 1951). The effort to involve, assist, and challenge student thinking through questioning provides a good illustration of a Safe for Thinking classroom and of cognitive instruction in practice. Kali thoughtfully structured questions to include the cognitive levels of the "Safe" model. He also used questioning purposefully to help students construct a knowledge base and to think with more complexity about it. He sequenced questions, built on students' responses, redirected questions for alternative answers, and used process questions to elicit more thoughtful interpretations. Kali's goal was to promote, sustain, and help improve the thinking of these sixth graders.

Beamon (1990, 1993) identified 20 such questioning practices from the cognitive research, and clustered them for observation purposes as shown in the Classroom Climate and Questioning Strategies model in Figure 5.1. The first seven practices address the opportunities a teacher gives for students to respond during a discussion. The four practices in the second part provide a means to identify the cognitive level on which questions are asked, based on the "Safe" model. The nine practices in the third section address a teacher's efforts to challenge students to cognitively process and thus respond to questions with more depth and complexity. Familiarity with these practices has helped teachers such as Kali to become more aware of how to use questioning strategically during inquiry-oriented discussion. Because young adolescents are fast developing the capacity for metacognition, it is important that they also recognize when they are involved in the kind of interaction that challenges them to become better thinkers.

---

1. *Response Opportunity*
   1.1 Teacher offers questions to class before specific students.
   1.2 Teacher accepts all valid student responses (nonjudgmental).
   1.3 Teacher gives sustaining feedback when needed.
   1.4 Teacher allows/queries for more than one student's point of view.
   1.5 Teacher elicits students' questions.
   1.6 Teacher permits students to answer other students' questions.
   1.7 Teacher distributes questions equably.

2. *Cognitive Level of Question*
   2.1 Teacher asks questions that help students set up the knowledge base (remember facts, make connections).
   2.2 Teacher asks questions that help students analyze new knowledge (interpret, infer, compare, explain).
   2.3 Teacher asks questions that help students focus knowledge in a new direction (predict, hypothesize).
   2.4 Teacher asks questions that help students evaluate new knowledge (judge, appraise, evaluate).

3. *Cognitive Processes*
   3.1 Teacher gives adequate wait time for cognitive level of question.
   3.2 Teacher's cognitive level of question elicits cognitive level response.
   3.3 Teacher pauses after students' responses (at least 3 seconds).
   3.4 Teacher asks probing questions for more extensive or complex responses.
   3.5 Teacher ask students to explain why or give proof for answers.
   3.6 Teacher asks follow-up questions at same or lower cognitive level.
   3.7 Teacher asks follow-up questions at higher cognitive level.
   3.8 Teacher asks students how they arrived at answer or to explain thinking.
   3.9 Teacher elicits higher-level questions from students.

Figure 5.1. Classroom Climate and Teacher Questioning Strategies
SOURCE: © Beamon (1990).

These practices were formally observed and documented in seventh- and eighth-grade language arts discussion during a 9-month study (Beamon, 1990, 1993). Students in classrooms where teachers used the practices more frequently showed higher levels of thinking expression than students in classrooms where teachers used the practices minimally. An analysis of these students' response patterns at the end of the study indicated increased elaboration, a better use of logic, and more detailed, unsolicited justification.

To understand better how these practices can be observed during a class discussion, the reader is invited to "slip" mentally into the back of Heather's ninth-grade English classroom. The climate is one of expectancy, interaction, and acceptance. Students had been asked to read the short story, *The Lottery* by Shirley Jackson (1966), in preparation for the current discussion; they had also been asked to write at least three personal questions related to the story. Although Heather had constructed her own questions, today she asked for a student volunteer to initiate the discussion (practice 1.5). Jay's question, posed to the group (1.1), was, "Why doesn't anybody in the village try to end the tradition of the lottery?"

Heather recognized Jay's A-level question (3.9), and paused (3.1) for the other students to think about possible responses (1.6). Jenny ventured, "It's kind of like clinging to a superstition for fear something bad might happen if you don't." Heather nodded (1.2), yet refrained from asking her for an example. The ensuing pause (3.3), however, seemed to compel Jenny to proceed: "You know, like lucky pennies or walking under ladders. Of course, that's not like human sacrifice, but maybe it's the same principle." Heather picked up the line of questioning with, "Would someone recall some facts in the story that indicate the tradition was becoming less prevalent?" (2.1). Several students volunteered instances, such as the mention of rumors that the village to the north had stopped the practice and the author's comments about the neglect of the black box and the elimination of much of the traditional ceremony. "Then why do you think they persisted with the annual lottery?" Heather rephrased Jay's initial question (3.7).

"I think it was a fear of change or maybe being skeptical of progress . . . like some people resist more liberal thinking 'cause it might corrupt society," Michael offered, quite insightfully. "Please explain your reasoning," Heather probed (3.5). Michael continued, "Well, one guy in the story, Old Man Warner I think (as he flips through the text) . . . yes, on page 6. . . . He calls the younger folks a 'pack of crazy fools' . . . the older generation seems to be clinging to the old way of thinking, and any change is like losing values." "Yes, I see what he means," volunteered Corrie. "We see it all the time today . . . one group accusing another of being too liberal." "Try to be more specific," Heather ventured (3.4). "Well, take the sex education issue. Think how much has been in the paper about how and what to teach in sex education classes. The state legislature even got into the act." "Good example," Heather acknowledged.

"Do you think it is human nature to be wary of change?" Heather posed an evaluative-level question (2.4, 3.7). "I do," spoke up Paula. "Especially, when it might go against a lifestyle or some really basic beliefs. I mean, all change might not be good. Who's to say? Just think about the debate over legalizing certain drugs."

"What about the need for change in the story?" Heather refocused the discussion. "In that case," Kelly responded, "I think change was needed, but the village was so isolated that communication was limited." Building on Kelly's answer, Heather posed a hypothetical question (2.3), "Speculate what would be needed in the story for the tradition of the lottery to end?"

What should be obvious to the reader in the preceding example is that the direction of an inquiry-based discussion can take many turns. The possibilities are numerous and often contingent on students' responses or the nature of the teacher's subsequent question. The technique, however, of stimulating student thinking remains consistent: varying the cognitive levels of questions, probing for cognitive processing, allowing time for thinking to develop, and providing ongoing opportunity for student questioning, response, and interaction. By being mindful of these strategies and by using them consistently, teachers can acclimate and accustom young adolescents to what good thinking involves, how thinking can be extended, and how to think about their own thinking. These process questions can help young adolescent learners move closely to higher standards for thinking quality. Some suggestions as to how teachers can determine when students' responses reflect improved thinking quality are discussed in the next section.

How to "Rate"
Students' Oral Responses

When teachers ask students questions, they generally anticipate responses that are correct or logical or thoughtful, depending on the cognitive level of the question. For knowledge-level questions, responses are easily recognized as correct or incorrect. When a student elaborates in response to a knowledge-level question, the answer is extended and usually richer in detail. To illustrate, contrast the following answers to the question, "Is there a boy in kindergarten named Charles?" No, versus no, his real name is Laurie. He's just making up the name so his parents won't find out he's causing all the trouble. The latter example would indicate, at least, a willingness to think and express beyond a monosyllabic response. (Of course, the student who gave the latter answer might have been in a "safe" classroom in which students were expected to "tell more.")

What about questions that attempt to elicit interpretive, hypothetical, or evaluative thinking? The reader might consider the following two student responses to the analysis-level question, "Why does Laurie invent Charles?":

To cover up for the bad things he was doing in school.
He could have been trying to let his mother know that he was having some adjustment problems at school.

The first response is plausible, one possible reason for the imaginary friend. The second response, however, attempts to offer some psychological insight into the situation (even if it puts a lot of faith in the motivation of 5-year-old Laurie!)

Another example of discernible differences can be seen in the following three responses to the teacher question, "How would we compare Laurie's behavior at home with Charles's behavior at school?"

It was like he was Charles instead of there being a Charles in the class.
Behavior at school was a lot more tense acting, like he wanted to get attention.
He played practical jokes at home. He started acting rebellious against his parents, and Charles was rebellious against the

teacher. He started trying to be a bigger person than he really was like Charles at school. His grammar deteriorated at home and it wasn't that great at school.

None of the three responses provides incorrect information; however, the latter two answers indicate an attempt to use the thinking skill asked for in the question—comparison. The third response obviously provides richer, more specific detail than the more general comparison offered in the second answer.

Because S-level questions are designed to elicit hypothetical thinking, the quality of student thinking behind the responses is challenging to assess. These questions open the door to speculation and student imagination. The reader is asked, however, to examine these responses to the question, "How would the story have changed if there really had been a 'Charles'?"

Well, maybe Laurie would have bragged about the trouble after school.

Well, Laurie's mom would have gone to the P.T.A. meeting and talked to Charles's mom and his mom would not have been satisfied until she talked with Charles's mom about his behavior.

For one thing, it would have solved the mystery about who Charles is. Laurie might have gotten worse . . . no, I change my mind, he might have gotten better after finding out the kind of trouble Charles got into once his mother had found out about what was happening at school.

The first response appears to involve some guessing on the part of the student; it certainly, in comparison to the other two examples, does little to extend the information in the story. The second and third responses do indicate some attempt to hypothesize based on the information in the story—thus one might argue, the students use some logical thinking to speculate about a change in events of the story. The reader is encouraged to notice, however, a difference in the third response. The student seems to be verbally reasoning through the speculation and attempts to make more abstract connections to the story's meaning.

An additional example of how a teacher might discern differences among students' thinking expression can be seen in the following responses to the evaluative-level question, "Would you consider Laurie a behavioral problem?"

> Yes, because he's doing things, like he hits people and the teacher and doesn't do what they say.

> Well, yes and no. Yes, because he was acting out a lot, playing lots of tricks . . . and no, because he just wanted to get attention and didn't get it at home or at a new school without many friends.

The first response judges the specific behavior at school and fails to offer any qualification that might explain Laurie's motivation. It reflects a more concrete, egocentric view of right and wrong behavior. The second, although less decisive, attempts to elaborate on possible motivation to explain the behavior by drawing parallels within the story text. If the question were asked later in a discussion after students had shared possible reasons for Laurie's actions, a teacher would hope to see a less judgmental stance. Young adolescents are developing a cognitive awareness that allows them to conceptualize the "delicate shadings" of right and wrong (remember Kate?). These cognitive skills, however, have to be nurtured, and inquiry discussion is one technique. The following rubric is based on criteria that can be used to assess the level of quality in student thinking expression:

Level 3:
- Specific textual clues provided with reference to topic
- Plausible, logical, and insightful explanation that links evidence to inference
- Rich detail supplied
- Unsolicited elaboration

Level 2:
- Correct information supplied but fairly general
- Fails to draw reference to textual clues
- Correct but no explanation or elaboration given

Level 1:
- No or incorrect response given
- Confusion of facts, meaning, or both

* Unsubstantiated guessing
* No relevance to question or issue

The preceding examples represent typical young adolescent responses. The reader can discern differences among the answers in the
level of insight, reasoning, and elaboration. A number of factors
could explain the differences: the knowledge of how to use the
thinking skill asked for in the question, the students' reading com-
prehension, or the developing ability to think more abstractly. The
stronger examples could also indicate that the students have had the
opportunity to articulate, practice, and improve thinking expression.

Understandably, the capacity for more abstract thinking varies
among young adolescent learners—all the more reason for teachers
to capitalize on this unfolding ability. If students respond with "I
don't know" to questions, teachers can offer assistance by rephrasing
the question, by supplying lower-level questions to build an understanding or by asking the student to reread aloud a passage that
contains clues for an answer. If students' responses appears impulsive or incomplete, teachers can probe or request support. With
guidance, young adolescents can thus gain confidence and skill in
thinking expression and begin to understand the teacher's expectation for better effort. And as teachers become more skilled at determining the quality of thinking reflected in students' responses, they
can better guide thinking development.

In Safe for Thinking classrooms teachers listen carefully to what
young adolescents are saying. They make critical and informed
decisions about what questions to ask, when to probe, how to follow
up, and how to build on student responses. They give students the
opportunity to express and practice thinking, they give them time to
think, and they value the ideas that students offer. They also establish
standards for increasing quality in verbal expression, expect students
to strive toward these expectations, and recognize when students are
progressing accordingly. In this context, young adolescents should begin to recognize what good thinking is and sounds like. Their oral
responses should become better formulated and reflect reasoning and
logic. They should be more willingly to offer elaborative support and
detail. They should also ask more questions and participate more
actively in class discussion. In this context, young adolescents should
become better thinkers.

How Can We Hold Students
Accountable for Learning?

Carolyn's classroom is often the topic of conversation in the teacher's lounge. A maverick at heart, Carolyn firmly believes that learning can be fun for young adolescents, and her classroom provides a "safe" environment for it. Students enjoy coming to class because they enjoy what they are doing, especially during the study of Egypt. They might work together in teams to plan an itinerary for a 5-day cruise on the Nile: finished products might take the form of travel brochures, interactive media demonstrations, and promotional skits. On other days, students might be seen sprawled on the floor of the classroom, painting hieroglyphic symbols into personalized cartouches. They reenact dramatic legends, such as the incarnation of the ancient god Amum-Ra or Hatshepsut's dream that led to her rule as one of the few female pharaohs in Egypt's history. They sport *gallabiyas*, personally designed from donated fabric and sample *aish shami* (white pita bread), hummus, *mahshi* (cabbage stuffed with rice), and *salata baladi* (a popular Egyptian salad of chopped tomatoes, cucumber, parsley, lettuce, cumin, and lime).

Common among the various activities and products is high student involvement, choice, variety, and relevance. Also characteristic is the element of student accountability. These seventh graders understand Carolyn's expectation for quality work, and they respond. As in the earlier examples, accountability in Carolyn's class translates into well-defined evaluative criteria. For example, at one point in the study, small groups of five students each were asked to generate a list of pros and cons of former Egyptian President Nasser's decision to build the Aswan High Dam. Pros might include the need for more sufficient water resources for the Egyptian people or satisfying the country's electricity needs or perhaps the inadequate control of silt by the old dam. The alternate perspective might include the loss of Nubian villages and changes brought to the area in rainfall patterns and level of underground water.

An ensuing discussion revolved around Egypt's dilemma in making the decision to sacrifice some of its property and cultural heritage to raise the current standard of living for its inhabitants. The discussion changed course when Brent (likely an aspiring museum curator or environmentalist) reminded everyone of the continuing problems in Luxor where the rise of salty ground water was eating away at the stonework of monuments. Carolyn seized the moment by asking the question: "Because you know what has happened in the wake of the High Dam's construction, both positive and negative. . . . Do you think man should use technology to change natural forces in the name of progress?" Students were asked to write a personal response in their journals, taking a stand on the issue raised by the question.

The following day Carolyn moved the students into different sets of five and assigned these group roles: archaeologists, economists, conservationists, politicians, and local citizens. The task was as follows:

Come to group consensus on the viewpoint of the assigned role about the wisdom of the Aswan Dam project. Prepare your argument for a debate.

Each group was subsequently asked to designate a representative to serve on the debate panel scheduled for the next day. What were Carolyn's evaluative criteria for this performance task? Continue into the next section for a glimpse in the classroom on the day of the debate.

Meaningful Assessment in
the Middle-Level Classroom

A rearranged classroom greeted the seventh graders on debate day. Two tables were positioned diagonally at the front with the podium, otherwise rarely used, situated in between. Teams were given 10 minutes for the selected representatives to review debate strategies before these designees took a seat at one of the tables. Carolyn moderated as the representatives alternated at the podium; time was given for counter-questioning from both panel and student audience. The politician representative spoke in favor of the wisdom of Nasser's decision to proceed with the project: It was a chance to support the progress and increasing self-reliance of a nationalized government. The archaeologists and conservationists spoke against the wisdom of the decision, pointing out the loss of numerous monuments beneath Lake Nasser and the environmental change in climatic conditions for the area. Interestingly, the citizen group took the stand in favor of the decision for progress, deciding that better electrical and water resources outweighed the ensuing environmental and cultural problems.

Evaluation of the debate focused on both content and process. Carolyn asked the students to select one of the representatives (other than their own) and to fill out the following evaluation form:

	Super	Good	Limited
Logical presentation of argument	3	2	1
Credibility of information	3	2	1
Persuasiveness of argument	3	2	1
Verbal delivery of speech	3	2	1
Involvement in counter-questioning	3	2	1
Comments or suggestions:			

The evaluation forms were given to the representatives, shared with their respective groups, and discussed in terms of how the debate arguments might be improved. Students followed up with a discussion of why the Western nations, led by the United States, refused support of the project, and the fact that Nasser turned to a willing Soviet Union to help finance the project. Carolyn asked the students to speculate on possible present-day repercussions in the area of international relationships as a result of America's decision not to support Nasser. The students were asked to respond in their journals to this question: Was the United States wise not to support the High Aswan Dam project?

Summary

Changing and expanded views of assessment have important implications for teachers of young adolescent thinkers. Current assessment methods focus on a check for understanding, application, and progress within the context of relevant, performance-based learning experiences. Group problem solving, simulation, audience-specific writing, and situations do more to reveal the depth of students' understanding than the traditional pencil-to-paper format. With its focus on the students' academic progress and cognitive growth, the new assessment philosophy renders a more "authentic" picture of student understanding, and has more potential for long-term learning and transfer. Meaningful assessment involves understanding where students are and can be encouraged to be, expected to be, and challenged to be along a thinking and learning continuum based on improvement and growth.

Meaningful assessment in the classroom can play an important role in the cognitive development of the young adolescent. Within the context of meaningful performance-based learning experiences, students can explore and experiment, and teachers can gain valuable information about their learning progress. Portfolios and "process-folios" allow teachers and students to keep "track" of ongoing progress as personal growth is evaluated and celebrated. Clearly communicated criteria for quality standards for thinking and learning can help students recognize where they stand in relation to the teacher's expectations, and toward which they need to strive to improve. The developing metacognitive capacity to reflect on and evaluate thinking quality helps students to gauge personal progress. Assessment used meaningfully and continuously to foster and guide the cognitive growth of young adolescents is an important element in a Safe for Thinking classroom.

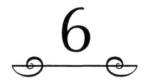

6

Extending for Meaning and Enrichment

"Why did the colors disappear?"

The Giver shrugged. "Our people made that choice.
. . . We relinquished color when we relinquished sunshine
and did away with differences."

"We shouldn't have!" Jonas said fiercely.

The Giver . . . smiled wryly. . . . "Close your eyes and
be still, now. I'm going to give you the memory of a
rainbow."

The Giver to Jonas, *The Giver* (Lowry, 1993, pp. 95-96)

Overview

How can teachers connect with the young adolescent's zeal for being and becoming, for knowing and experiencing? The "magicians" who have tend to offer similar strategies for what and how to teach students, ages 10 to 14. Center a curricular unit around a theme and help students make learning connections across content areas. Give students an opportunity to discuss current issues and delve into problems that directly affect them. Encourage students to explore and develop interests. Build on students' strengths. Focus on opportunities that help students become self-directed learners. Give students some choice in what and how they learn, and in how they express learning. Use technology and community resources to link students to the real world.

Strategies that extend the basic curriculum and enrich the cognitive development of young adolescents are the focus of Chapter 6. Numerous classroom scenarios illustrate how thinking can be challenged through thematic exploration, extended learning connections, and the creative use of instructional technology. A collaborative multimedia project among students, teachers, and a media specialist is highlighted in a scenario that stretches young adolescent learning experiences beyond the traditional classroom setting.

Linking Content With Thinking Processes

Young adolescents need content that is meaningful to think about. They also need to learn to think more extensively about more complex content. Tomlinson (1995, p. 8) has specified three essential elements of curriculum with which teachers in all classrooms deal. These are (a) content, or what students are expected to learn; (b) process, or how they relate to and cognitively "make sense" of ideas and information; and (c) product, or how they demonstrate their learning. In the illustrations throughout this book, young adolescents have been learning content in a "building block" fashion: gathering new information, making sense by connecting new information with familiar cognitive structures, and thinking about the new learning in a more complex fashion. When young adolescents initially acquire new knowledge, their minds work for a basic understanding. When these primary connections are formed, they can begin to consider more intricate relationships and patterns among the pieces of information. Teachers need to help young adolescents make the "elementary" connections; they must also challenge students to extend their thinking about the more abstract content for their cognitive skills to develop and improve.

When teachers expect young adolescents to consider content-related issues, problems, and themes, they are challenging these students' thinking to progress to increasingly higher levels. This approach also critically parallels and supports these young thinkers' developing cognitive capacity to process the more abstract ideas. The following example illustrates the expectation for a student to think with increasing complexity about increasingly complex content:

> Determine the physical characteristics of each stratum of a rain forest.
>
> Reason why specific wildlife inhabitants are adapted for living within the various strata of the rain forest.
>
> Speculate about repercussions on life in a Costa Rica rain forest should a major land development project be permitted to proceed with the building of a golf resort on adjacent acreage.
>
> Formulate your position as a member of a community chamber of commerce asked to review the company's proposal to build the resort.

The first example requires that students gather fairly specific content. The second example, in contrast, requires analytical reasoning to determine a relationship within the information. In this case, students would need to draw connections between the inhabitants' adaptive traits and the particular characteristics of the habitat. The third illustration further challenges students to consider hypothetical implications in a real problem situation. In the fourth situation, student thinking extends further as they are challenged to evaluate information related to such abstract issues as economic development and the conservation of natural resources.

The progression of thinking moves from lower to higher (recall the "Safe" questioning model from Chapter 4), and the content from basic understanding to more intricate situations. The lower level is important as a building block for information processing; however, teachers need to challenge young adolescents to "stretch" their thinking capacity beyond this basic level. The previous illustration shows the way a teacher might connect content and process in an increasingly complex way to extend the level of student thinking. Consider another example in reference to a study of Native Americans. If the teacher wants to help young adolescents gain a basic understanding of the stressful conditions along the Trail of Tears, he or she might ask any of the following:

> Trace on a modern map the route of the Cherokee Indians along the Trail of Tears.

Compute the number of miles walked per day on the Trail of Tears.

Describe the hardships suffered by the Cherokee Indians along the Trail of Tears.

Give reasons why Andrew Jackson forced the displacement of the Cherokee Indians.

To extend thinking to the A-level, however, and to have students consider content of a more complex nature, the teacher might present the following challenge:

Compare the plight of the Cherokee Indians to that of the Jewish population as described in *The Diary of Anne Frank* (Frank, 1989) (previously read by the class).

Analyze Andrew Jackson's reasons for ordering the displacement of the Cherokee Indians.

Infer from the reading how the Cherokee Indians must have felt when forced to leave their homes for an unknown land.

Identify other instances in history when diverse cultures have clashed to the disadvantage of one population.

In these examples students are challenged to make connections, see relationships, examine assumptions, and draw inferences from the content. Their thinking is expected to extend beyond a basic understanding level. The content is also more complex because students are thinking about feelings, human motivation, and similarities among related information. In the latter instance, the content deals with the abstract theme of cultural diversity; anticipated student thinking, however, remains on the interpretive A-level.

Should the teacher's purpose be to extend student thinking in a new or different direction, she or he might ask students the following:

Think of an alternative resolution to the political reasoning that led to the displacement of the Cherokee people.

Predict the impact on today's Cherokee population had Native American leaders and government representatives been able to reach an alternative arrangement.

These thinking and learning expectations parallel the F-level of thinking in the "Safe" model. Student thinking calls for a more creative, problem-solving approach as students deal with alternatives to real-world situations.

Thinking at the evaluative level poses a genuine challenge to young adolescents. Consequently, teachers need to provide opportunities for students to practice this kind of thinking before the content becomes too complex. For example, students might be asked to evaluate the reasons for the displacement of the Cherokee Indians in terms of a political perspective. They might be asked to appraise the decision in terms of the human rights issue. More complex content could be introduced with the following challenge:

> Formulate your opinion about maintaining English as the national (and only) language of the United States.

The previous examples reflect various ways in which what students learn can be extended and how students think about new information can be challenged. Developmentally, young adolescents are acquiring the cognitive skills to think more abstractly about more complex material; nevertheless, they need time and assistance to make the transition from concrete to more formal thinking. The progression can be continuous, but rarely is it in a "quantum leap" fashion! And even with the acquisition of higher thinking capacity, most young adolescents need assistance to comprehend and assimilate new information before they try to think about it in a complex manner. A teacher has to be "tuned in" to what students know and understand, and to when they are cognitively "ready" for more in-depth thinking and more challenging content.

Curricular Themes and
Real-World Connections

Is there a "magic formula" for motivating young adolescents learners? Consider for a moment the class of 10-year-olds who contrasted current lifestyle with that in the early 1900s. They interviewed a classmate's great-grandmother, examined microfiche documents in a community library, and analyzed tombstone rubbings from a turn-of-the-century cemetery. The theme was culture, and the study coincided with the local community's bicentennial celebration. The ceremonial opening of the courthouse cornerstone spurred students to fashion personal time capsules that reflected present lifestyle: These were stored away in safe places with strict instructions regarding an "opening" date. A student-directed video documentary complete with fashion, music, and pastimes portrayed the lifestyle of 10-year-olds growing up in the local community early in century. Oral history, action research, and a high level of personal involvement helped these young adolescents conceptualize the events that influence and shape a community's culture.

Consider the group of 12-year-olds who speculated about the impact of a recent Middle East political election on world trade relations. The discussion generated from the class's exploration of the theme of global interdependence. The seventh graders had collected information on current world events from the media and Internet, had monitored developments in peace talks, and had followed the power-struggle saga of world leadership. They debated, composed, and mailed position papers to eminent national figures on issues of economic sanction, foreign investment, and labor management. Student "delegates" in appropriate dress role-played an international summit to explore feasible solutions for ongoing world conflict. The event was covered by the local newspaper. These young adolescents learned via current events, simulation, and problem solving about the complex economic, political, and cultural interplay of global decision making.

Were these students motivated to learn? Were they challenged to think? Absolutely! Young adolescents become excited about learning that is current and relevant, and they are motivated to learn when they get actively involved. The students in these examples gathered information from a variety of real-world sources and connected it within a framework of more complex and broader issues, problems, and themes (Kaplan, 1979). Learning that takes place within a relevant and purposeful context is more meaningful, more likely to be internalized, and more likely to last.

The preceding scenarios show how learning experiences can stimulate the cognitive development of young adolescents. The students are involved in collaborative research, inquiry-based discussion, and problem solving. They are expected to gather, analyze, and synthesize pertinent information. Ideas need to be formulated thoughtfully and communicated purposefully. By assuming the viewpoints of past and present figures, these young adolescents stretch their developing cognitive capacity to understand the world through a perspective other than their own. These students are relating to pertinent issues about which they literally have a voice. Within the context of abstract themes and real concerns, these young adolescents are trying to understand and explain the complexities of human nature.

What curricular themes are relevant for the young adolescent learner? A teacher need only consider what is related to these students' developmental needs—independence, exploration, conflict, interdependence, power, survival, relationships, honor, justice, expression, communication, change, courage (Beane, 1992). The list could continue. Young adolescents are fast developing the cognitive capacity for abstraction. What better way to captivate their interest than through the discussion of concepts important to their daily existence? Themes, in addition, provide a broader "scaffolding" for basic information and skills specific to state- or system-adopted curriculum (Howard, 1996). Basic content is mastered but in the more comprehensive framework of relevant problems, key issues, and abstract themes. Teachers' creativity lies in the way they construct challenging and meaningful learning experiences that help students relate within a more complex level of content.

Thematic Planning and Young Adolescent Learning

The theme of survival was the "connecting framework" for a unit developed by Lacy, a popular sixth-grade teacher. Students read the Paulsen (1987) novel *Hatchet* about the young teen who survived in a mountain wilderness after a plane crash. They applied social studies skills through analysis of story descriptions and the design of topographical, climatic, and directional maps. They integrated mathematics by estimating food rationing and figuring percentages of rainfall, and language arts through response journaling and composition. They also discussed the survival theme in other novels previously read. These young adolescents, in addition, researched the "science" of edible wildflowers and other life-sustaining flora, and planted a wildflower garden off the terrace of the art studio. The tragic deaths of a party of mountain climbers in east Africa prompted a class project to design survival guides for safe climbing across rough terrain at high altitude.

In planning for the study, Lacy questioned what she wanted the young adolescents to learn specifically about the theme of survival—in other words, what was her ultimate purpose for its selection? The sixth graders had been among the first students to attend a newly constructed middle school, and had experienced a predictable share of adjustment pains. A different organizational pattern and changes in peer formations had accompanied the usual and daily confusion of young adolescence. Accordingly, Lacy formulated the following basic generalization: Survival often depends on knowing and applying useful information to meet a person's needs. As part of the unit, the students conceptualized what "survival" had meant to them as new students and decided what information and skills had been needed for the transition. These "veteran" sixth graders then sponsored an orientation night for rising sixth graders . . . complete with skits, tours, and humorous flyers on "maintaining your cool"—or survival at New Garden Middle. Lacy taught specific content and basic skills in related subject areas. She also successfully helped these students think abstractly about the content and conceptually about their personal development as young adolescents.

An eighth-grade teacher explored the theme of cultural diversity through the study of Native Americans, content that was similarly specific to the state-adopted social studies curriculum. His goal was to help the young adolescents develop an understanding of and stronger respect for differences and similarities among people. He formulated the following basic generalization: A better understanding among cultural groups promotes communication and respect. Students identified problems between early settlers and Native American groups, speculated how the conflict could have been managed more peacefully, and role-played the resolution. They researched rituals and customs, read legends, and studied cultural traditions. They created dances to reflect their understanding of legends and produced an original dramatic opera, complete with costumes, to convey an understanding of tribal customs.

These young adolescents also considered personal assumptions about Native Americans and discussed how misconceptions were perpetuated. They examined textbooks and literature for evidence of stereotyping and inaccurate presentation of information. These eighth graders related to the content on a more personal level by creating dream catchers to reflect their personalities, designing totem poles to represent personal belief systems, and constructing a symbolic alphabet to reflect the values of their present-day culture (Maker, Nielson, & Rogers, 1994).

The true test of these young adolescents' understanding of the theme of cultural diversity came when they were challenged with modern situations in which cultural differences caused communication barriers to understanding. The students identified instances in which they were directly affected by cultural misunderstanding, prejudice, and bias. A panel discussion evolved around the philosophical issue of whether cultural identities should and could be preserved, such as through ethnic celebrations and self-contained communities, or if cultural diversity should and could be minimized and assimilated more into the mainstream of American living. The discussion also extended to cultural differences that engendered major conflict throughout the world. Through this study, these young adolescents also dealt with another prevalent concern, the search for personal identity.

Young adolescents are dealing with multiple concerns, and as Kate at the beginning of Chapter 4 indicated, they are asking a million questions about who they are and how they relate to others and the world around them. They are dealing with physical, social, and psychological changes as they are trying to determine a personal identity and their place in the immediate, extended, and global communities. These youngsters are fast developing the cognitive structures to think abstractly about issues and concerns that touch their lives daily. A thematic approach to teaching content enables young adolescents to express and deal with their concerns in the context of a Safe for Thinking classroom.

Another advantage of a thematic approach in the teaching of content is the opportunity for multiple learning experiences. Gardner's (1983) multiple intelligence theory was evident in the description of the eighth-grade Native American unit, for example. Students learned and expressed learning through verbal-linguistic, visual-spatial, logical-mathematical, musical-rhythmic, body-kinesthetic, and inter- and intrapersonal avenues. They wrote, speculated, debated, discussed, composed, sang, acted, interacted, and reflected. The thematic approach, in addition, enables teachers to integrate various content areas into a study, as in Lacy's study of the theme of survival.

Had Lacy been teaching on an interdisciplinary team, she and her colleagues might have collaborated to teach to the selected theme. Survival, for example, can be seen in the world of science through plant and animal propagation; in the economic area, through the concepts of competition, supply, and demand; in the literary world, in which characters find themselves in conflict with nature; or through real-life mathematical problem solving, such as in estimating rations for rain forest exploration, in calculating fuel demands for an intercontinental flight, or in graphing food shortages in Third World countries on the computer. In this approach, the generalization might be this: Survival is based on certain characteristics that enable continuation.

A thematic approach to teaching content gives young adolescents a framework for connections that can reinforce, extend, and enrich their learning. Student thinking is engaged through meaningful, relevant, active, and multiple learning experiences, and cognitive structures are strengthened. Young adolescents have the opportunity to consider real-world issues and problems about which they need to be and are concerned. They are motivated, excited, and willing to give their best effort; simultaneously, they are developing and practicing skills for abstraction and higher-order reasoning. In tandem with consistent and ongoing assessment, thematic teaching can help young adolescents become more proficient thinkers. Various and multiple ways through which young adolescents learn and meaningfully show their learning are explored in the next section.

Where Does Performance Fit In?

Performance-based products, as indicators of student learning, have been discussed in terms of assessment in Chapter 5. Products are the third piece of the curriculum puzzle (Kaplan, 1979; Tomlinson, 1995). Products require students to "fashion" information into new and, at times, creative formats (Gardner, 1993). Gathering bits of information about one side of an issue, for example, takes on new meaning for students when they "transform" the information into a debate. Creating a dramatic opera, as in the Native American study, challenged eighth graders to synthesize content into an original production. Products reflect the application and expression of student learning, and can help teachers assess student understanding and progress.

Products, in addition, bring choice to the learning situation as teachers allow young adolescents to connect with personal interests and explore through multiple intelligences (Gardner, 1993). Many examples of musical, written, visual, problem solving, performance, group and individual products have been provided throughout this book. The debates, for example, draw on interpersonal, verbal-linguistic, and logical-mathematical skills. Artistic products, such as the totem pole, dream catcher, or costumes in the Native American unit, encourage the exploration of intrapersonal and visual-spatial intelligences. The various problem-solving scenarios give expression to skills of verbal communication, logical reasoning, and personal reflection. Other products, such as legend reenactment, dramatic role play, dance, and musical composition involve kinesthetic movement and rhythm.

The possibilities are numerous. Teachers who run out of ideas need only to ask their students as one sixth-grade teacher did. The young adolescents eagerly brainstormed over 100 ways to present their learning. Some of their ideas included the following: write a riddle, a cryptic message, a fairy tale, or a suspense drama; make a junk sculpture, a mural, a matrix, or a mixed-media collage; stage an impersonation, a comedy routine, a skit, or a mock trial; fashion a learning game, a comic strip, a children's book, or a graphic design; create a video, a commercial, an advertisement, or a multimedia presentation; or design a banner, a bumper sticker, a travel brochure, or a computer game. Certainly young adolescents will be more motivated as active learners involved in projects of their own choice and design.

No matter how creative a product is, it has limited meaning unless it is appropriately linked to the content and the anticipated thinking level (Howard, 1996). The rain forest examples in the earlier section can be used to illustrate this relationship among content, process, and product. Take another look.

Determine the physical characteristics of each stratum of a rain forest.

Reason why specific wildlife inhabitants are adapted for living within the various strata of the rain forest.

Speculate about repercussions on life in a Costa Rica rain forest should a major land development project be permitted to proceed with the building of a golf resort on adjacent acreage.

Formulate your position as a member of a community chamber
of commerce asked to review the company's proposal to
build the resort.

In the first example, students could possibly record the characteristics of the strata in labeled columns on charts or artistically
represent the information on posters. Either product would demonstrate a basic understanding as students translate factual information
to a different format, that is, from source to chart or poster. They
could also describe strata characteristics verbally. A creative product,
such as a banner or a travel brochure advertising an expedition
through the rain forest, might be fun for young adolescent students
but seems unnecessary in the check for basic understanding of rain
forest strata!

In the second situation, the teacher could ask students to show
an understanding of how the information is connected through a
classification matrix or other graphic organizer. In the third learning
situation, students might choose among such products as a group-
generated list of consequences, a protest letter, descriptive poetry, or
a musical composition. The final example lends itself more appropriately to a position speech, an editorial to the local newspaper, or a
role play of a simulated community meeting.

Multiple and varied performance products are possible in the
Native American study example, but once again, teachers of young
adolescents need to bear in mind the purpose of the product. Useful
questions might be, What is it about this content that I want students
to know? What kind of thinking do I want reflected? How best can
students demonstrate this understanding to me? A few sample products are suggested with the examples below:

Compute the number of miles walked per day on the Trail of
Tears. (computer bar graph, simple calculation)

Describe the hardships suffered by the Cherokee Indians along
the Trail of Tears. (brief role play, reenactment, descriptive
story)

Compare the plight of the Cherokee Indians to that of the Jewish
population as described in *The Diary Anne Frank* (Frank,
1989). (Venn diagram, character dialogue, discussion)

Infer from the reading how the Cherokee Indians must have felt when forced to leave their homes for an unknown land. (dramatic monologue, poetical response, mixed-media collage, small group discussion)

Formulate your opinion about maintaining English as the national (and only) language of the United States. (letter to a politician, speech from the perspective of a Mexican immigrant, simulated dialogue)

The examples of performance products in this section extend the content and level of thinking in meaningful ways. Many of the examples connect with real-world concerns, allow students latitude in selection, and accommodate for multiple intelligences. Opportunity is also given for collaborative and independent work. In Chapter 5, the importance of ongoing assessment was emphasized, but it was also noted that all performance products do not have to be graded. It is important, however, that students know specific evaluative criteria so they can concentrate their efforts toward increasingly better performance. In a Safe for Thinking classroom, curriculum content extends learning into more complex and relevant situations, the thinking process engages and challenges, and the performance-based products express genuine learning and understanding. The following set of questions are useful criteria for developing content, process, and performance products that enrich the learning experiences of young adolescents and help improve thinking capacity:

Does a thematic approach provide a broad and connecting framework for facts and related information?

Is the content complex enough to challenge reasonably and relevant enough to interest?

Is there chance for students to connect new learning with what they know?

Are students expected to process the content on different and varying thinking levels?

Do students have a chance to deal with current issues and problems that directly affect them?

Is there occasion for student choice and exploration of interests?

Are there opportunities for collaborative group work?

Are there chances for individuals to direct learning independently?

Are there multiple and various ways through which students learn and express their learning?

Are standards for student learning products clearly communicated?

Are avenues provided for learning connections beyond the classroom?

An additional question might be, Has technology been incorporated into the learning experiences? The instructional use of technology to extend and enrich the learning of young adolescents is explored later in this chapter.

Dealing With All Those Interests and Abilities

Thinking about curriculum in a way that allows for extension and enrichment also helps teachers meet the diverse range of abilities in a typical class of young adolescent learners. Some students will learn grade-level content quickly and will need to move quickly to a more complex level. Others will come to class already knowing the basic content whereas some will struggle to make even the most rudimentary connections needed to establish a basic knowledge base. Some students will have strong interests in science fiction, and others in graphic design. Some may have strengths in mathematical problem solving, some may have a flair for dramatics, and others may be talented musicians. Some may be well traveled, motivated, and goal oriented, whereas others may bring limited experience and resource. Some may enjoy learning but are easily bored, whereas others who are easily bored may dislike anything about school. What's a teacher to do? Make decisions that respond to different learning needs and interests, and stay flexible.

Dave's seventh-grade math class provides an example of the way teachers can challenge the diverse thinking and interest levels of young adolescents. Some of Dave's students needed practice with more basic operations, including percentage, whereas others were ready for probability and geometric calculation. Determined to meet these diverse needs without resorting to teaching to the middle level,

Dave used a problem-solving format that allowed students to apply various levels of math skills (Lane Education Service District, 1983; Marchioni, 1988). Students were presented word problems about realistic situations and asked to work individually or in teams to solve the tasks. The problems were constructed to require an application of learned and new math skills, and no particular "prescribed solution" was anticipated. They were expected, however, to share strategies, to evaluate their effectiveness and to create additional problems to challenge classmates. These seventh-grade students also created their own mathematical problems with data they collected from the Internet, various almanacs, statistical records, newspapers, journals, and consumer reports. A sample problem follows:

1. Five seventh-grade friends (three male and two female) decide to attend a rock concert at Stoney Creek Amphitheater. Tim's dad's van maintained a speed of 60 miles per hour until he hit a stretch of traffic that slowed him down to 45 miles per hour for 30 minutes. They were late for the 7:00 show. What time should they have left home? If the concert ended at 11:00 p.m., how late would it be when they returned home?

2. Tim and Michael both have a crush on Katie. If Tim's dad gives the tickets out randomly, what is the probability either will get a seat next to her? What is the probability they will get seats on each side of her? What is the probability Katie will not want to sit beside either of them?

3. During the concert intermission, Tim's dad has a conversation with the person in the seat next to him about the money collected in concessions at the concert. If the 30,000 people attending each bought a soft drink, what would the site business gross if each drink cleared 20% profit? How much would be made if one third of those attending the concert bought a souvenir cap and one half bought a T-shirt at the same profit percentage?

4. If Tim's dad decided to invest in the T-shirt industry for the group's next concert, what kind of profit would he realize if given 7% dividend? If he invested his profits at 6% compounded interest, how many years would it take Tim's dad to gross 1 million dollars?

5. As a tribute to the performers, a group of students on the lawn decided to stand hand-in-hand to form a circular chain on the grassy knoll. If they succeeded in shaping a complete circle with a diameter

of 25 feet, how many students would be in the formation? What size square would this same number of students be able to form? Could they form an equilateral triangle? What size hexagon could they form?

The parts of the previous problem vary in math skill application and level of difficulty (basic operations, probability, percentage, basic geometry). It is also apparent that pertinent information is missing in several places, causing the need for students to gather, construct, or hypothesize about the data. In the case of Question 1, for example, students must estimate the time getting out of the parking lot, for Question 4, they have to speculate about attendance at a future concert, and for Question 5, they must determine the average arm span of students typically attending a rock concert. Each part calls for application of the problem-solving skills, including collection and examination of data, hypothetical reasoning, calculation, and conclusion.

Dave's students worked together to solve different parts of the problem and enjoyed creating new problem questions to challenge classmates. During the follow-up sharing session, the seventh graders shared problem-solving strategies, evaluated the techniques, and discussed ways to improve these skills.

Erin and Margaret deal with the multiple abilities and interests of their sixth graders through flexible grouping. Although not "officially" on a team, these teachers of similar philosophy decided to form a teaching partnership. Students moved from room to room and into the larger multipurpose room, depending on what structural arrangement these creative teachers had in mind. During a study around the theme of symmetry, for example, students explored concept in the natural world, in geometric design, in musical composition, and in poetical arrangement. Whereas some students were challenged by the task of recognizing symmetrical patterns, others were asked to create their own. Some of the students composed musical and poetic stanzas, created their own tessellation, and designed original computer graphics. All students were expected to gather information about symmetry in nature during a nature walk; one group, however, decided to take photographs with a digital camera. They demonstrated how to manipulate the images on the classroom computer.

Erin and Margaret varied the composition of student groups as needed to meet the challenge of particular tasks. For example, in the study of the rain forest, they discovered some students were very knowledgeable of the strata characteristics, were ready to tackle the issue of progress versus conservation, and soon had gathered enough data to offer a solution to a problem of their own invention. Other students, however, needed a stronger understanding of the relationship of the various strata before effectively debating the issue. Of course, management of all this "flexible activity" was a feat for even these energetic teachers. They believed firmly, however, that this kind of "strategic differentiation" was necessary to keep active young adolescents motivated and challenged.

Teachers of young adolescents share the important responsibility of capitalizing on an emerging and novel capacity to understand abstract relationships and make personal connections. They have a prime opportunity to help students consider, discuss, and think with increasing complexity about meaningful content within a "safe" classroom context. Because young adolescents bring diverse learning needs to the classroom, teachers also have to make decisions about the complexity of the content and the level of the thinking appropriate. Although teachers need to help students make foundational learning "connections," they also need to challenge continually so student thinking will develop, extend, and improve. Through this intellectual challenge, young adolescents can begin to build the cognitive structures for future decision making, ethical responsibility, and personal accountability.

Young Adolescent Writers at Work

Nancie Atwell (1987, 1990) links the process of writing with the young adolescent's need to explore, to express, to delve, to think, and to understand. Elements such as guided instruction, drafting, response, conferencing, sharing, collaboration, goal setting, evaluation, and publication support the philosophy that young adolescents need a "safe" environment to develop cognitively, socially, and psychologically. They need direction, for example, and they need to feel it's okay to feel a little uncertain about where they are headed. They need opportunity to pursue ideas of personal interest and to improve skills within specified writing tasks. They need support in the form of encouragement, constructive feedback, and audience. They also need expectation in the form of limitations, rules, and evaluation. It's all about balance, one eighth-grade teacher reflected: "Don't leave out the freedom but don't go overboard on ownership."

How can the writing process be an effective tool to foster the cognitive development of young adolescents? Again, the answer lies in the terms, *process* and *progress*. Young adolescents' heads are filled with ideas and thoughts, worries and concerns, dreams and plans. Teachers can stimulate these ideas and generate others through strategies that include literature response, imaginary mental journeys, or discussions that range from current events to the abstract concepts of hurt, death, fear, or loneliness. It is foundationally important for young adolescents to transfer their ideas and thoughts onto paper—any size, any color, and any texture—because these ideas become writing possibilities. Students may or may not choose to experiment with these literary "seeds"; the thinking processes of valuing and evaluating, however, begin as these ideas are collected, sorted, and considered.

Young adolescents also need to realize that writing does not have to be paragraphs on lined paper. Students can design limericks, campaign slogans, advertisements, tall tales, and script; they can fashion poems, children's books, journals, and jokes; they can form cryptic messages, memoranda, word games, songs, and letters; they can create menus, computer programs, brain teasers, and word problems; they can write lists, directions, recipes, captions, and reviews; and they can make statements, express opinions, take a stand, write proposals, predict an event, describe a dream, and defend a belief. The possibilities for the written word are limited only by students' imaginations and the teacher's willingness to let writing happen in the classroom.

A structured writing workshop can give young adolescents many other opportunities to practice their developing metacognitive and evaluative skills. Students generally set writing goals and are held accountable to them through class status records, sharing sessions, teacher conference summary forms, structured peer evaluations, and personal reflection. Each of these strategies helps young adolescents to monitor personal progress and think about the improvement of writing skills. When students are allowed to select personal ideas for optional writing pieces, they feel a sense of ownership; when they respond to assigned writing tasks, they learn specific modes of rhetoric.

Throughout the writing process, the expectation is for improvement. Accountability and celebration come together during the publication stage. Whether spoken from an author's chair during a poetry reading, printed in the school or local newspaper, shared with younger students, e-mailed to pen pals, featured in a portfolio on parent night, or bound in a literary journal, the writing of young adolescent students needs to be validated. They feel a spirit of pride in an accomplished task that has also been done well.

Well, that's the way it should happen, provided all goes well! As one teacher readily admits, staging a writing workshop with a class of eighth graders can be a "management nightmare" (M. Armstrong, personal communication, July 9, 1996). Sometimes young adolescents realize they can "dodge" the accountability notion and actually "hide" in the structure. Interestingly, this avoidance game is possible because of a new cognitive capacity to manipulate. The result? No product and no progress. Again, young adolescents need to understand the process, the evaluation criteria, the expectation for progress, and the anticipated level of performance. And again, this means meaningful and ongoing assessment. The student mind-set should be, "I'm doing well. I've done well. I'm doing better. I can get better." The teacher mind-set should be, "I see value in your ideas. I see improvement in your skills. Keep at it. You're getting better, but you can get even better." Support, opportunity, and expectation make a writing workshop approach a Safe for Thinking instructional strategy.

Exhausting? You bet, according to this teacher who manages the writing workshop format year-to-year with 30-odd eighth graders. Rewarding? Again, yes. Consider these comments from one of his students: "I've never thought of myself as a writer. No one has ever told me I had talent in poetry until now. I'm going to keep on writing."

Any other tips about writing for teachers of young adolescents? Consider the following strategies from a veteran writing teacher:

Allow students the freedom to tap into their interests.

Use writing to connect with other content areas, especially social studies.

Don't get too caught up in the self-concept thing. Accountability is important. Get kids beyond giving lip service to writing.

Help students realize the value of all their ideas . . . these may be the most brilliant ones when developed.

Creativity can be extended within the process of writing.

Let students know they've done well but that they can do better.

Help students to recognize what good thinking looks like on paper.

Skills have to be taught.

Sounds like valuable advice in helping young adolescents become better writers—and better thinkers.

How Technology Can Be a "Turn-On" to Learning

The scene is a meeting room at a state-level education conference. A group of youngsters, ages 11 to 14 squirm restlessly on aluminum chairs; two teachers and a media specialist pace the floor as the room slowly fills with conference participants. The equipment has been checked and double-checked; the handouts are ready. Tension breaks somewhat as the group is introduced and the multimedia presentation begins. What had motivated this group of young adolescents to share their time and energy with a roomful of strangers? What has motivated them to give up a Saturday and travel across the state in a van with their teachers? Technology, of course, and the chance to use it for learning!

The opportunities for teachers and students to learn with instructional technologies are mind-boggling. In school systems across the country, buildings are being wired and classrooms connected. Electronic mail links young adolescents with potential classmates, with pen pals in other countries, and experts in various fields. Students are communicating with younger students, college students, and the elderly. Information access is so quick, easy, and bountiful that students are literally overwhelmed with what to use and how best to use it. A 13-year-old can find out where his favorite music group is performing, what it costs, and directions to get there. This same youngster can link through Internet with a mentor in an astronomy research lab, an international museum, industrial sites, or weather stations. Teachers are networking to share curriculum ideas and strategies that work, integrating multimedia into classroom instruction, and managing complex data and image processing projects.

Hyerle (1996) used the term *interactivity* to describe this new relationship between students and information access. Exciting advances in instructional technology provide young adolescent thinkers with unlimited possibilities for research and problem solving. The skills of the fast-advancing technology age are no longer limited to packaged programs and computer-directed learning because countless opportunities are available for authentic learning and young adolescent high-level thinking. In classrooms across the world, students are telecommunicating, collecting data, accessing, digitizing, downloading, scanning, manipulating, sharing, questioning, graphing, mapping, analyzing, reasoning, and creating.

Imagine the excitement of seventh graders who, in a study of African culture, share data about the level of acidity in the rainwater of Zambia. Imagine the motivation of fifth graders who track the migration of geese from Canada to Florida; who share and collect data about the acidity of acid rainfall in various parts of the world; or who dialogue with archaeologists, zoologists, or agriculturists about ancients cultures, animal habits, or soil analyses. With a computer, the appropriate software, and modem capability, young adolescents can interact with specialists and other adolescents internationally to solve real-world environmental problems, to investigate weather patterns, or to examine solar energy intensity (Bradsher & Hagan, 1995; Solomon, 1989).

The multimedia conference presentation described earlier in this section is another example of the collaborative use of technology. Several young adolescents, their teachers, and the school media specialist had been involved in several technology projects. The three 8th-grade boys had created an interactive video demonstration on the literary elements of Lois Lowry's (1993) *The Giver* (instead of the traditional book report). The two 6th-grade girls had combined recordings, computer imagery, and personal commentary for a multimedia research project on the Beatles. The other students had worked with one of the teachers to prepare an interactive video presentation on Gardner's (1983, 1993) multiple intelligences theory. Another of the teachers, as a graduate class project, had designed an interactive technology project to heighten awareness among fellow teachers of the instructional value of young adolescent fiction. He surveyed students for their favorite titles, and analyzed the setting, character, plot, and theme of each book selected. The final product was displayed in the school media center.

The group was encouraged to present the various multimedia projects at a state education conference. Their presentation focused on motivating students to learn through technology, and is another example of how teachers can extend young adolescent thinking and learning beyond the classroom.

Slip back into that conference meeting room where the session is underway. The teachers have given a brief overview and rationale for the presentation, and provided explanation of the various assignments. The media specialist has given an explanation of the more technical aspects of the project, namely the capabilities of the software package, memory requirements, and the necessary hardware for the interactive display. When the students, ranging in age from 11 to 14, take center stage, they literally steal the show. These young adolescents are obviously excited at the opportunity to demonstrate the multimedia projects, and they "wow" the audience of educators with their enthusiasm, knowledge, articulation, and self-confidence. They appear comfortable talking about the conceptualization of the projects and willing to elaborate on the steps of preparation. The test of credibility comes, however, when the audience is allowed to ask questions. Where are these inquiries directed? The adults step aside and the students close the 90-minute session with utmost poise. With the presentation over, however, their seriousness dissipates and young adolescent laughter can be heard down the convention hall escalator as the group heads for the nearest pizza parlor.

How can teachers tap into the powerful resources of technology? Easy. Information is readily available about a variety of online network projects, and many districts are providing training opportunities for teachers to learn program and project management. Computer competency tests are becoming required for young adolescents and prospective teachers. In some instances, teachers are being required to renew licensure, at least partially, through technology training. School districts are investing huge sums of money into software and supporting hardware. Educational technology is definitely in the limelight as educators are beginning to realize its potential for student thinking and learning. With instructional technology, young adolescents can explore relevant problems, practice inquiry, math, science, and communication skills, understand and learn more complex content, and sharpen thinking.

Technology and young adolescents are a natural combination in the Safe for Thinking classroom. Whether writing about their interests with peers in distant places through electronic mail, gathering data for projects from the Internet, collaborating on exploratory science projects, creating intricate imagery, learning through simulations and virtual reality, or working cooperatively on multimedia presentations, young adolescents are actively developing, using, and improving an array of thinking skills. They are learning to tap current information sources beyond the local setting, to process data, and to use information in a purposeful and challenging way. These youngsters are also networking in a world of unlimited dimension, a global society within which they will soon live as adult learners. Technology used in instruction is important in fostering cognitive competence in young adolescents. Technology enriches young adolescent learning and extends their thinking beyond the classroom. Does technology motivate learning? Ask any young adolescent!

Beyond the Middle-Level Classroom

It is 7:15 a.m. A few teachers move slowly through the building. The school has altered little structurally since Miss Howell's teaching days . . . an expanded media center, a couple of classrooms converted to computer labs, a renovated gymnasium. A series of administrators, a steady flow of youngsters, and the usual turnover of teachers marked the 30-odd years. A new school philosophy. A different organizational pattern. A younger, more sophisticated student body. The lower eighth-grade hall appears unchanged. Striding swiftly through his classroom doorway, the teacher almost trips over the bodies of two students asleep on the carpet (M. Armstrong, personal communication, July 9, 1996).

"Hi, guys," the teacher greets the boys, his expression reflecting no surprise. These two had been waiting for him almost every morning for the past 2 weeks, eager for extra time to work on their technology project. The regular school day never seemed enough and they had so many ideas they wanted to try. Besides, the project due date was near.

What motivates young adolescents to give up morning sleep for school work? Well, this project has been no ordinary assignment. The sleeping boys were part of a three-person team working on an interactive media presentation. The project went on to win second place in a statewide technology contest in which these eighth graders competed with teams of students in grades 8 through 12. The extra time paid off for the students. There were other payoffs as well. One of the young men has decided to be a film maker, admitting to the teacher that "he'd never had the confidence until this class."

Student involvement and enthusiasm for learning are characteristic of this Safe for Thinking classroom. The opportunity for collaborative learning is common as students with varying abilities, skills, and interests pool personal resources to complete group tasks. Probably Mike's most popular assignment is the I-search project in which students select an area of interest, formulate questions about it, and conduct concentrated research to find out the answers. From in-line skating to the Delta blues the topics range, and for one month the students literally "live" the assignment. They access the Internet, read, interview, listen, and write. "We become a real community of learners," Mike reflected as he describes how the use of technology brings the students together. "Whenever students run across any information about a classmates' project, they download it and print it out!"

The end products are in the form of oral presentations, and they have proven to be the most creative this educator had seen over several years of teaching. One student, for example, wrote a 30-page research paper on the evolution of African American spirituals into the blues. He demonstrated the transition through the music itself, alternating line for line the original spiritual and the blues selections. Another student learned to use her dad's film-editing equipment for a very polished showing. "This project gives kids a chance to do something wonderful and beautiful and terribly creative," Mike still spoke with awe. "It was a high point as a teacher." And this is the man who had recently received the system's highest honor for his teaching!

How does he grade these projects? "It goes way beyond grades," he grins. Sure, he and the students establish criteria for performance: His expectations for quality are high and his standards specific. The students, however, are given free rein to direct their own learning about a topic of personal interest and they are challenged to demonstrate their learning in a way that makes most sense to them. Mike comments on the quality of thinking reflected through the various projects—the array of multiple intelligences, the inquiry, the analysis, the synthesis, the creativity, and the personal reflection: "I am able to sit back and be amazed." Mike's classroom is a "safe" place for young adolescent thinking to develop.

Summary

Teachers as classroom decision makers share a responsibility to provide the kind of curriculum and instruction that stimulates student thinking and motivates long-term learning. Marzano (1992) has expressed that "the ultimate purpose of learning is to use knowledge in meaningful ways" (p. 15). Young adolescents are developing the capacity to think about information on a level beyond the mere shuffling of facts and dates. They can and should be challenged to think about pertinent issues, real-life problems, and abstract themes and concepts that directly affect their daily experience. They also need practice in applying their ideas to new and novel situations. Extension and enrichment of the curriculum through more complex content, more challenging process, and more meaningful learning performance helps teachers meet the needs of young adolescent learners.

Scales (1991) reported that students, ages 10 to 14, possess a developing capacity to care about humanistic issues that affect their lives, yet this potential tends to diminish when left unnurtured. Schurr (1989) has recognized the potential of young adolescents to form values and make responsible decisions, yet is concerned that these students are intellectually "at risk" without developmentally responsive teachers. Whether discussing the pros, cons, and reasons behind China's one-child policy, the lingering racial strife in South Africa, or a local effort to cut a major thoroughfare through a nearby residential area, middle level students can begin to formulate and understand the complexity of current issues, to formulate strategies for solution of real-world problems, and to explore, discuss, and write about abstract themes that relate to their personal development.

Technology has opened the door of the traditional classroom, and through its use, students gain the power to direct their own learning. Technology has the potential to extend student learning through speedy and direct information access, to extend student communication with peers and mentors, and to extend student creativity through multifaceted project development. Through technology, young adolescents can solve problems, share resources, and build networks. Collaborative technology projects connect students to the larger educational community through research and service. Technology puts young adolescent thinkers in touch with a global society within which their decisions will one day be valuable. Technology also offers teachers unlimited resources to integrate thinking and instruction. Technology promises to extend the experiences of the "safe" classroom into another dimension of learning and thinking for young adolescents.

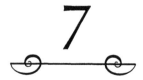

7

Anticipating the Challenge Ahead

We shall not cease from exploration
And the end of all our exploring
Will be to arrive where we started
And know the place for the first time.

"Little Gidding,"[1]
Four Quartets (T. S. Eliot, 1943, p. 59)

Overview

One of the greatest gifts teachers can give their students is a belief in the capacity of their own minds. Miss Howell instilled this belief in that fortunate group of young adolescents many years ago, and they, now practicing professionals and parents, appreciate and celebrate this gift. Memories of her classroom are still vivid, and adult conversations frequently return to those seventh-grade days of exploration, challenge, and personal growth. Miss Howell's expectations were high and challenging, yet she provided a "safe" place for young adolescents to think, to learn and, in turn, to know themselves. Miss Howell believed in her students, and this belief continues to inspire.

Teachers of young adolescents face a greater challenge than those of Miss Howell's generation. Moving into a new century, today's teachers carry the weight of diminishing parental involvement, a more prevalent substance abuse problem, and the premature sophistication of an age group struggling with the transition from childhood to young adulthood. Society's problems have no respect for the closed classroom door. Today's young adolescents live in a world of easy access, and they are forced to make decisions before they are prepared to consider the ramifications. These young people are coming-of-age in a society characterized by mass communication and massive information flow, and their future role in it will be an important one.

Teachers of today's young adolescents also educate within seemingly paradoxical circumstances. They are expected to prepare students for a rapidly changing global society in which the skills of reasoning, analysis, evaluation, and reflection are critical; yet they find themselves accountable to stringent curricular guidelines and narrowly focused assessment measures. Classrooms are populated by a widely diverse group of learners, yet support systems vary from fair to minimal. Many teachers feel overwhelmed with change and perplexed at how to "fit in" all they are expected to do. Most acknowledge the importance of technology, for example but are challenged to find the time to use it meaningfully with instruction. And there are all those other expectations.

A dismal picture of the educational scene? Yes. Any hope in sight? Yes, again. One of the goals of this book has been to help teachers realize that they have control over important decisions that directly influence the thinking and learning of their students. The purpose of Chapter 7 is to reiterate some of the ways teachers can create a Safe for Thinking environment in which young adolescents can develop and thrive. Teachers are reminded that new understandings from the cognitive and young adolescent development theories are workable within the framework of what they do best— teach. Teachers of young adolescents are encouraged to learn, to grow, and, in some instances, to change direction as the new century unfolds. The culminating scenario is a dream of what can be. It is also a glimpse of what must be.

Education at the Crossroads

The philosophy of this book supports the author's belief that educators today live in the "best of times." Despite the external pressures of fluctuating public confidence, bureaucratic governance, and tightening accountability, and regardless of the internal pressures of motivating and teaching a diverse group of young people, the possibilities for meaningful classroom dynamics are apparent. The conditions are favorable for change, and indeed, many improvements are underway: Several changes, however, still need to be made. Education is at a critical crossroads, and educators now know enough about student thinking and learning to move in the "right" direction.

Several factors have favorably shaped the current educational climate. A serious consideration for worthwhile living in the new century has rekindled an interest in thinking development. Meaningful participation in the society of the new millennium will require the ability to think critically about significant problems and issues, to discern discrepancy, to formulate perspective, to support viewpoints with logic, to tolerate diversity and dissonance, and to evaluate personal growth. These thinking skills are important for productive living in a global society: They are also critical in the cognitive development of the young adolescent.

Underlying the renewed focus on young adolescent thinking development is a growing emphasis on active involvement, self-directed learning, individual accountability, group collaboration, extended learning opportunities, and continuous improvement. The thrust is not merely on teaching students the skill to think but on setting the standards for them to learn to think better. Whether articulated, written, or reflected in various performances or products, the current discussion about thinking revolves around talk of progressive and developmental criteria based on standards of quality. The emerging cognitive theory-into-practice has the potential to transform the traditional classroom into a dynamic, interactive, and thinking-conducive learning environment.

The language of learning measurement similarly has begun to move away from the previously characteristic terminology of *norm-referenced* and *standardization*. Questions have been raised about the "authenticity" of traditional measurement, and phrases such as "meaningful assessment," "levels of performance," "evaluative criteria," and "standards for quality" are more common in the vernacular of educators. A trend has begun across the United States to assess student learning and understanding within or as close to the actual learning experience as possible. The growing use of problems-based instruction is evident across multiple disciplines and on varying grade levels. Furthermore, students themselves have become more knowledgeable of the indicators of thinking levels and actively participate with teachers and peers in the evaluation of their own thinking and learning.

The cognitive research has further provided educators with a clearer picture of the functioning of the human brain during the thinking and learning process. Teachers have a better understanding of instructional strategies that facilitate information processing and those that impede. An enlightened understanding about the interactive and developmental capacity of intelligence has opened new avenues for student learning and its expression. Connective to these theories is the strong emphasis on a stimulating and interactive classroom environment in which students have multiple and varied opportunities to learn and to demonstrate their understanding. These theories, in addition, have precipitated a wealth of curricular and instructional ideas to assist in the teaching of students in the 10 to 14 age group.

Furthermore, teachers of young adolescents are encouraged that emerging cognitive theory makes sense within the framework of day-to-day classroom operation. To teach thinking does not have to mean adding a new subject, learning a new curriculum, or sitting through another training session about a new instructional approach. It does mean, however, a different way of looking at the way teachers and students interact, the way standard curriculum is developed and taught, and the way understanding is measured. The cognitive research is clear that active learning stimulates young adolescent thinking, that appropriate challenge motivates it, and that meaningful, ongoing assessment supports and improves it. These conditions characterize the Safe for Thinking classroom.

Moving in the Right Direction

Current cognitive theory has helped teachers of young adolescents better conceptualize the classroom conditions favorable to the thinking and learning process. Converging with this enlightenment about student thinking is the continuing national focus on young adolescence as a distinctive period of human development. A newspaper columnist recently questioned, "tongue in cheek," why so much attention has been given to young people in the 10-to-14 age group: During the first part of the 20th century, this population was virtually nonexistent! A plethora of reports and journals in this field of study, fortunately, has helped to communicate that young adolescents are in need of a unique kind of classroom instruction.

Some important parallels can be drawn between young adolescent developmental needs and thinking instruction. Young adolescents, as tentative explorers of thinking, are receptive to the opportunity to try out emerging cognitive abilities, but they can be easily discouraged by unreceptive teacher actions. They are simultaneously delighted in and awed by the new capacity to think abstractly and metacognitively, yet they tend to be their own worst critics. Furthermore, although young adolescents need something meaningful to think about, they also need assistance both in acquiring a basic knowledge base and in understanding the different levels to which their thinking can aspire. Young adolescents' thinking can improve when they understand what "good" thinking is and when they know they are getting closer to what is expected.

Young adolescents themselves seem to be paradoxical in nature. Amid accelerated social, emotional, and cognitive change, these young people are yearning for direction, defying authority, and seeking the answers to a multitude of unanswered questions about everything from why hot water freezes faster than cold, if indeed it does, to how to kiss properly, if indeed there is a way. They need both guidance and freedom, direction and choice. Young adolescents represent the hope for a future generation, and what happens in the classrooms of today is pivotal.

It is important that teachers of young adolescents recognize their power to make critical decisions about the nature of classroom interaction and instruction. Young adolescent learners respond to opportunities to share their ideas, to explore developing opinions, and to experiment with new thinking capacities. Recall the fun of composing a limerick for the first time, even if it was about the girl with the red hair in the seat in front or the boy who always graded your vocabulary words. Young adolescence is a time when potential can be likened to a burst of colorful fireworks against a night sky. Exploding interests and ideas, frenzied concerns and worries, a rainbow-blast of ups and downs, stops and starts. Young adolescents need the freedom to be who they are and the encouragement to become who they can be and are. They also need the challenge to be the best they can be. Creating a classroom climate in which young adolescents feel "safe" to grow, develop, and stretch is a powerful and imperative step in helping these students develop and strengthen cognitive skills.

Learning through inquiry-based discussion, thematic units, research, writing workshops, collaborative group projects, simulations, problem solving, debate, performance, role play, creative dramatics, online telecommunication, community projects, and multimedia presentations provides young adolescents a chance to "try out" expanding cognitive abilities in an active learning context. Teaching for thinking, however, involves a philosophical shift in what and how teachers of young adolescents teach. Teachers can no longer presume the role of authority in the classroom: There is simply too much to know and too many other ways to find it out!

A popular humorist once noted that young people enter school as question marks and exit as periods, certainly a sad statement on life in classrooms. What punctuation mark might characterize the energetic spirit of young adolescent students? An exclamation point might symbolize their sense of wonderment about everything from personal sexual awakenings to human rights in China. These students are fascinated by new phenomenon and intrigued by the unusual. They want to be acknowledged as teenagers, yet cling to the security of childhood familiarity. Their developing capacity for empathy can be seen in genuine concern for the impact of such global problems as poverty and hunger. Young adolescents are yet unscathed by adult disillusionment and believe with staunch optimism that their voice can make a difference in the quality of life for future generations.

Meaningful learning during the young adolescent period is foundational to living meaningfully in a new century. Helping these students acquire and strengthen their developing cognitive skills is the goal of meaningful instruction in Safe for Thinking classrooms. The following scenarios capture the spirit of creating the best possible learning environment for young adolescent cognitive development.

The Dynamics of the
Future Middle-Level Classroom

Step into the school where Judy and Bruce, two ninth-grade teachers are collaborating on instruction around the theme of cultural expression. Judy teaches a course in world cultures and Bruce teaches art. They hope students will gain an understanding that art is often the expression of a culture's beliefs and values. Groups of students gather data about the art forms of periods in various cultures, including African batik, Egyptian papyrus designs, Chinese silk watercolors, European Impressionist period oils, and early American primitive paintings. Students "visit" museums via Internet and download sample prints. They research the art forms and determine what various techniques and subject matter reveal about specific cultures.

These young adolescents also bring in actual prints of artwork from parents' travels, communicate by electronic mail with national and international museum curators, and fashion computer graphics. The groups determine what style, color, media, and texture indicate about a specific culture. Students visit local museums, interview artists, and conference with art historians at the nearby college. The groups are responsible for an interactive presentation that reflects what they learn about cultural expression through art. The students incorporate text, digital imagery, graphics, dialogue, sound effects, and music into sophisticated performances.

Across the courtyard is Dayna's seventh-grade classroom where curious and energetic 12-year-olds are busy at computers. In the past, Dayna's request to take out math or science textbooks had been accompanied by unmuffled groans, especially among some of the female students. In the past, Dayna has also been perplexed as to the best way to include several students with limited English proficiency. How to teach planetary astronomy had this recent college graduate baffled until she figured out a better way to make the study meaningful—to even the most reluctant seventh-grade learner.

Look more closely and notice that the school is networked for online access, and teachers like Dayna are accustomed to its use. Several digital cameras are available in the media center, and teachers have been trained to use a variety of public domain image processing programs. Dayna is involved in a collaboration project with her former college physics professor who teaches a research-based astronomy course. The project has been overwhelmingly positive, so far. Dayna paired language-challenged students with language-proficient classmates and each team was linked with a college partner. Even students who had struggled with English have begun to talk more confidently, and even the most reluctant students are beginning to show unprecedented enthusiasm for math and science.

In Dayna's classroom 12-year-olds and 19-year-olds communicate regularly through electronic mail, sharing questions and ideas about the solar system and planetary astronomy. The seventh graders have been studying images of the solar galaxy, of planet configurations and satellites, and of various planetary surface features. They have solved and written mathematical problems in which they applied curriculum-specific content skills. The college students are currently using advanced image processing to study geological structures on the surface of Venus, and have shared their data with Dayna's students. The college researchers (Raphael & Greenberg, 1995) have explained in detail how they calculated the diameter of volcanoes on the planet's surface and classified these according to size. One recent clear evening, middle-level and college students went to a local observatory and photographed Venus with a telescopic lens. Afterward, a group of the more precocious 12-year-olds created their own digital images, which they in turn demonstrated for fascinated classmates.

Intrigued by reports of past life on Mars, the seventh graders have begun to gather all the available information they can find from the Internet and other sources, printed and written. They have studied images of Mars's surface conditions and communicated electronically with NASA scientists to explore the hypothesis. They intend to continue telecommunications with the "expert" older students, even after the college term has ended. They also have "big plans" for an exciting culmination to the study: Several of Dayna's students will join the college students at a campus research forum where they will copresent on image processing.

What is Dayna doing? She's walking around among the students asking question after question. She's also learning, too. Listen to some of her questions. Why do scientists propose life has existed on Mars? What is the basis for your hypothesis? How can you test your ideas? What evidence have you found that might support your theory? What makes you think that the information is reliable? How would you describe the surface of Venus in mathematical terms? How is the surface of Venus comparable to that of Mars? How would you describe the configuration of the planetary system to a six-year-old? How could you calculate the diameter of any of the planets? What mathematical operations would help you find the diameter of any of the small volcanoes on the surface of Venus? Why is Mars called the "red planet"? Why are scientists so interested in finding indications of life on other planets? Dayna is as excited as the seventh graders themselves because she knows that thinking and learning are happening in her classroom. When two of the female students, who had been initially so adverse to math and science, ask to design a children's book about the mathematics of space travel, for extra credit, of course, she flashes that familiar grin.

Down the hall in Tom's technology class something different is happening. In fact, his students are not even there! These ninth graders have collaborated with system administrators who are concerned about the attrition rate of area students to private schools. These students have designed a video for the local cable station that will feature the "good things" about the public schools in the district. They have photographed computer and science labs, sporting events, teacher-student projects, and many examples of student involvement as the "selling points" of the video. Currently the students are out in the school interviewing other students, media specialists, and support staff, which they will incorporate into the script.

Tom realized early in the year that his eighth graders knew more about using technology than most teachers in the school. Experienced with the Internet, scanners, digital cameras, image and data processing, and graphic design, these students had planned and conducted a technology demonstration workshop for teachers in the system. Are Tom's students motivated? Are they involved in real-world projects? Does Tom find ways to extend and enrich the learning experiences for his students? Is his classroom a Safe for Thinking environment? The answers are obvious. By the way, Tom has recently received national financial support for another community collaboration project.

In another part of the building teams of fifth and sixth graders are getting ready for "performance day." Two classes have assembled in the multimedia room where small groups will present original interpretations of the modern-day implication of fairy tale themes. Jennifer and Anne, to better meet the ability and interest needs of students in their classes, often cluster students in groups across the two grade levels. Instead of reading and discussing the themes of several fairy tales, the teachers decided to take a different approach (Jacobs, 1994). They are emphatic about wanting their students to think more independently, to make decisions about their learning, to explore their talents, to work more effectively in groups, and to experiment with a variety of performance products. The following is the task they assigned:

> Form a group of 3 to 5 classmates. Select a fairy tale, determine its theme, and create a 20-minute multimedia presentation about the message in modern-day terms. Use multiple media, art, other literature, sound, visuals, and performance to create an original production.

Anne and Jennifer let the students form their own groups, although they cautioned them to think about members who could bring differing talents to the task. They had suggested that the students spend a few minutes initially thinking about what strengths they personally had to offer. For example, who could design visuals? Who had a special knack for dramatic performance? Who was a good organizer or a good note taker? Who were the technology "experts"? What kinds of other talents did anyone possess? What were their interests? They then let students mill around in the larger classroom and "shop" for a group. Both teachers were amused at how candidly the students represented themselves to each other. The selection process had continued during one lunch period, after school, and by telephone that night. By the next day, tentative groups had been formed, and by the subsequent day, most groups had decided on a fairy tale. Interestingly, many of the groups included mixed ages.

Jennifer and Ann also had spent a large block of time talking with students about the evaluation process. They had explained that each group would be given a grade based on the following criteria: creativity, variety of media, organization and shared contribution, and quality of final performance product. They accepted students' ideas about the criteria and reminded them that peer evaluations would, as usual, follow the final presentations. At check points during the 2-week work time, group members had been asked to evaluate the progress and overall effectiveness of working together. Each student had kept a journal of what the group members had accomplished during the work periods; each had also reflected on how to improve quality and productivity.

The teacher team acted as advisers and facilitators, but these students were ultimately responsible for the planning and "staging" of the productions. Students were challenged to use their best resources, to collaborate purposefully, and to be creative. After a few rocky starts, some disputes about how to narrow ideas to the 20-minute format, and the expected round of last-minute jitters, the groups were ready to perform and the teachers were ready for a treat. So were school administrators and several rows of faithful parents, grandparents, and younger siblings.

Look again into the multipurpose room because the first presentation had begun. Stage lights flash and a flourish of music from a popular screenplay sounds as the curtain goes up on three students in black leather jackets. This trio entertains the audience with a few dance steps before pausing abruptly at the (taped) sound (effects) of a motorcycle. The gang leader arrives, his hair spiked and colored and his outfit, hideously mismatched. As it turns out, he has just had a "makeover" at the local salon. The humorous skit on this rendition of "The Emperor's New Clothes" continues until one of the students gathers the courage to level with his friend about his unsightly appearance. The skit ends as the students are joined by the light technician in an original choreographed dance routine.

The next presentation is a pantomime of "Cinderella." Peers make fun of a classmate at a party because she does not know how to dance. With the secret help of the friendly disk jockey, however, she arrives at the next dance and surprises them all by demonstrating a new dance. Of course, she forgives their snobbery and new friends exit arm in arm. Other presentations follow that involve a multimedia slide show, an animation, a video presentation, and a poetry reading with musical accompaniment. Perhaps the most moving performance comes when a new Japanese student presents a dramatic monologue about the challenge of adjusting to a different culture. Two other members of his group have designed stage scenery that depicts a scene when the "ugly duckling" is ostracized because of its physical differences. The presentation ends with a digitized panel show of multicultural classmates in various scenes in and out of school. A third student plays John Lennon's "Imagine" on her saxophone in the background. The proud group receives a standing ovation from the audience.

The young adolescents in the preceding scenarios are active learners and challenged thinkers. They are involved in meaningful learning experiences that connect them with a world beyond the classroom. They are given both choice and direction, freedom and structure. They are interacting, exploring, and experimenting. They are also gaining a better understanding of who they are and how they relate to their world.

Summary

The education of young adolescents is at a critical crossroads. The convergence of recent cognitive research and young adolescent developmental theory at a time when thinking has been conceptualized in terms of quality performance has strong implication for teaching students ages 10 to 14. This new and potentially powerful understanding, however, must be translated more commonly into practice. Teachers of young adolescents need to teach in the way their students learn best, and this may mean changes in the way some teachers operate classrooms. The best instructional practice for young adolescent thinking and learning means allowing them some choice in how they learn and in how their learning is expressed. It means allowing these students to think about pertinent issues, current problems, and relevant themes. It means giving up tight control over a class discussion but still expecting students to work at improving the thinking level of their responses. It means involving students in collaborative learning groups and allowing them to set evaluation criteria for products. It also means learning how to use technology, connecting students with "outside teachers," and facilitating community action projects.

Teaching, learning, and thinking in the 21st Century must be responsive to a new global society defined by interaction, activity, and change. The new millennium promises unfathomable advancement in technology, communication, and information access. To impact with any significance on the quality of living, young adolescents will need a keen sense of the concepts and values that will guide personal choices and determine responsible decision making. The skills of reasoning, analysis, valuing, and evaluation will be basic to productive living. Teachers of young adolescents must meet the challenge to provide the opportunities that will help prepare young adolescents for a meaningful existence. Young adolescents also need to feel confident that the skills they acquire will carry them forward as the leaders, thinkers, and learners of a new age. The following popular rhyme celebrates this young adolescent spirit:

You have brains in your head.
You have feet in your shoes
You can steer yourself any direction you choose.
Step with care and great tact
and remember that Life's
a Great Balancing Act.
And will you succeed?
Yes! You will, indeed!
(98 and 3/4 percent guaranteed.)

OH, THE PLACES YOU'LL GO! (Dr. Seuss, 1990).[2]

Notes

1. Excerpt from "Little Gidding" in FOUR QUARTETS, copyright 1943 by T.S. Eliot and renewed 1971 by Esme Valerie Eliot, reprinted by permission of Harcourt Brace & Company.

2. From *Oh the Places You'll Go!* by Dr. Seuss Enterprises, L. P. Reprinted by permission of Random House, Inc.

References

Alper, L., Fendel, D., Fraser, S., & Resek. (1996). Problem-based mathematics—Not just for the college-bound. *Educational Leadership, 53*(8), 18-21.

Armstrong, T. (1994). *Multiple intelligences in the classroom.* Alexandria, VA: Association for Supervision and Curriculum Development.

Atwell, N. (1987). *In the middle: Writing, reading, and learning with adolescents.* Portsmouth, NH: Boynton/Cook.

Atwell, N. (1990). *Coming to know: Writing to learn in the intermediate grades.* Portsmouth, NH: Heinemann.

Barell, J. (1985). You ask the wrong questions! *Educational Leadership, 42*(8), 18-23.

Beamon, G. W. (1990). *Classroom climate and teacher questioning strategies: Relationship to student cognitive development.* Unpublished doctoral dissertation, University of North Carolina at Greensboro.

Beamon, G. W. (1992-1993). Making classrooms "safe" for thinking: Influence of classroom climate and teacher questioning strategies on level of student cognitive development. *National Forum of Teacher Education Journal, 2*(1), 4-14.

Beamon, G. W. (1993). Is your classroom "SAFE" for thinking?: Introducing an observation instrument to assess classroom climate and teacher questioning strategies. *Journal of Middle Level Research, 17*(1), 4-14.

Beane, J. A. (1992). Turning the floor over: Reflections on a middle school curriculum. *Middle School Journal, 23*(3), 34-40.

Beyer, B. K. (1987). *Practical strategies for the teaching of thinking.* Boston: Allyn & Bacon.

Bradbury, R. (1980). All summer in a day. In *The stories of Ray Bradbury* (pp. 532-536). New York: Alfred A. Knopf.

Bradsher, M., & Hagan, L. (1995). The kids network: Student-scientists pool resources. *Educational Leadership, 53*(2), 38-43.

Brophy, J. E. (1986). Teacher influences on student achievement. *American Psychologist, 41,* 1069-1076.

Bruner, J. (1964). The course of cognitive growth. *American Psychologist, 19*(1), 1-15.

Caine, R., & Caine, G. (1991). *Making connections: Teaching and the human brain.* Alexandria, VA: Association for Supervision and Curriculum Development.

Carnegie Council on Adolescent Development. (1989). *Turning points: Preparing American youth for the 21st century.* Washington, DC: Author.

Carroll, L. (1971). *Alice in wonderland.* New York: W. W. Norton.

Clark, B. (1983). *Growing up gifted* (2nd ed.). Columbus, OH: Charles E. Merrill.

Costa, A. L. (1985). Teacher behaviors that enable student thinking. In A. L. Costa (Ed.), *Developing minds: A resource book for teaching thinking* (pp. 125-137). Alexandria, VA: Association for Supervision and Curriculum Development.

Dahl, R. (1979). The landlady. In *Ronald Dahl's tales of the unexpected.* London: Joseph.

Dewey, J. (1933). *How we think.* Boston: D. C. Heath.

Dillon, J. T. (1981). To question or not to question: Questioning and discussion. *Journal of Teacher Education, 32*(6), 51-55.

Dillon, J. T. (1982). The effect of questions in education and other enterprises. *Journal of Curriculum Studies, 14*(2), 127-152.

Eliot, T. S. (1943). *Four quartets.* New York: Harcourt, Brace & World.

Elkind, D. (1984). *All grown up and no place to go: Teenagers in crisis.* Reading, MA: Addison-Wesley.

Ennis, R. H. (1987). A taxonomy of critical thinking dispositions and abilities. In J. Baron & R. Sternberg (Eds.), *Teaching thinking skills: Theory and practice* (pp. 9-26). New York: W. H. Freeman.

Frank, A. (1989). *The diary of Anne Frank.* New York: Doubleday.

Franquet, S., & Sattin, A. (1996). *Fodor's exploring Egypt.* New York: Fodor's Travel Publications.

Gall, M. (1984). Synthesis of research on teachers' questioning. *Educational Leadership, 42*(3), 40-47.

Gallagher, J. J., & Gallagher, S. A. (1994). *Teaching the gifted child* (4th ed.). Boston: Allyn & Bacon.

Gardner, H. (1983). *Frames of mind: The theory of multiple intelligences.* New York: Basic Books.

Gardner, H. (1991). *The unschooled mind: How children think and how schools should teach.* New York: Basic Books.

Gardner, H. (1993). *Multiple intelligences: The theory in practice.* New York: Basic Books.

Glenn, H. S., & Nelson, J. (1991). *Raising self-reliant children in a self-indulgent world.* Rocklin, CA: Prima.

Good, T. L., & Brophy, J. (1984). *Looking into classrooms* (3rd ed.). New York: Harper & Row.

Good, T. L., & Brophy, J. E. (1990). *Educational psychology: A realistic approach* (4th ed.). New York: Longman.

Haglund, E. (1981). A closer look at the brain as related to teachers and learners. *Peabody Journal of Education, 58*(4), 225-234.

Hart, L. (1975). *How the brain works.* New York: Basic Books.

Hart, L. (1983). *Human brain and human learning.* New York: Longman.

Hart, L. (1986). A response: All "thinking" paths lead to the brain. *Educational Leadership, 43*(8), 45-48.

Homer. (1946). *The odyssey.* London: Penguin.

Howard, J. (1996, February). *Designing curriculum for diverse learners.* Paper presented at the annual meeting of the American Association of Colleges for Teacher Education, Chicago, IL.

Hyerle, D. (1996). *Visual tools for constructing knowledge.* Alexandria, VA: Association for Supervision and Curriculum Development.

Jackson, S. C. (1951). Charles. In R. M. Stauffer, W. H. Cunningham, & C. Sullivan (Eds.), *Adventures in modern literature.* New York: Harcourt, Brace & World.

Jackson, S. (1966). The lottery. In J. Moffett & K. R. McElheny (Eds.), *Points of view: An anthology of short stories* (pp. 556-565). New York: New American Library.

Jacobs, R. (1994). Letting go: A multimedia poetry project. *English Journal, 83*(6), 70-76.

Johnson, D. W. (1976). *Jack and the beanstalk.* Boston: Little, Brown.

Jones, B. F. (1986). Quality and equality through cognitive instruction. *Educational Leadership, 43*(7), 5-11.

Kaplan, S. (1979). *Principles of a differentiated curriculum for the gifted and talented.* Los Angeles: National/State Leadership Training Institute of the Gifted and Talented Curriculum Council.

Keyes, D. (1959). *Flowers for Algernon.* New York: Harcourt, Brace & World.

Kozol, J. (1994, November). Quotation referenced in a paper presented at the 41st annual convention of the National Association for Gifted Children, Atlanta, GA.

Lane Education Service District. (1983). *Problem solving in mathematics.* Palo Alto, CA: Dale Seymour.

Lazear, D. (1991). *Seven ways of teaching: The artistry of teaching with multiple intelligences.* Palatine, IL: IRI/Skylight.

Lazear, D. (1994). *Multiple intelligence approaches to assessment: Solving the assessment conundrum.* Tucson, AZ: Zephyr.

Lee, H. (1960). *To kill a mockingbird.* New York: Warner.

Little, J. (1986). *Hey world, here I am!* New York: Harper & Row.

Lowry, L. (1993). *The giver.* New York: Bantam.

Maker, J., Nielson, A., & Rogers, J. (1994, Fall). Giftedness, diversity, and problem solving. *Teaching Exceptional Children,* 4-19.

Marchioni, G. (1988). *Mathematical adventures in decision-making.* Princeton, NJ: Woodrow Wilson National Fellowship Foundation Mathematics Institute.

Marzano, R. J. (1992). *A different kind of classroom: Teaching with dimensions of learning.* Alexandria, VA: Association for Supervision and Curriculum Development.

Marzano, R. J., Pickering, D. J., & Brandt, R. S. (1990). Integrating instructional programs through dimensions of learning. *Educational Leadership, 47*(5), 17-24.

McBride, R. (1992). Preparing the physical education environment for critical thinking. *Inquiry: Critical Thinking Across the Disciplines, 10*(2), 12-13.

Merrill, J. (1978). *The pushcart war.* New York: Dell.

North Carolina Education Standards and Accountability Commission. (1995, July). *Second annual report to the North Carolina State Board of Education, the North Carolina General Assembly, and Governor James B. Hunt, Jr.* Raleigh: State of North Carolina Office of the Governor.

Nummela, R., & Rosengren, T. M. (1986). What's happening in students' brains may redefine teaching. *Educational Leadership, 43*(8), 49-53.

Paul, R. (1994). What are intellectual standards? *Educational Vision: The Magazine for Critical Thinking, 2*(1), 10.

Paul, R. (1996, May). The practical impractical. *Education Week,* pp. 30, 32.

Paul, R., & Elder, L. (1994). Critical thinking: Using intellectual standards to assess student reasoning. *Journal of Developmental Education, 18*(2), 32-33.

Paulsen, G. (1987). *Hatchet.* New York: Puffin.

Purkey, W. W., & Novak, J. M. (1984). *Inviting school success: A self-concept to teaching and learning* (2nd ed.). Belmont, CA: Wadsworth.

Raphael, J., & Greenberg, R. (1995). Image processing: A state-of-the-art way to learn science. *Educational Leadership, 3*(2), 35-37.

Reilly, D. H. (1995). *How to have successful schools!: What parents and teachers need to know to improve children's learning.* Lanham, MD: University Press of America.

Rowe, M. B. (1971). Wait time and rewards as instructional variables, their influence on language, logic, and fate control. Part one—Wait time. *Journal of Research in Science Training, 11*(3), 84-94.

Rowe, M. B. (1986). Wait time: Slowing down may be a way of speeding up! *Journal of Teacher Education, 37*(1), 43-50.

Scales, P. C. (1991). *A portrait of young adolescents in the 1990s: Implications for promoting healthy growth and development.* Chapel Hill: University of North Carolina, Center for Early Adolescence.

Schurr, S. L. (1989). *Dynamite in the classroom: A how-to handbook for teachers.* Columbus, OH: National Middle School Association.

Seuss, Dr. (1990). *Oh, the places you'll go.* New York: Random House.

Shaw, G. B. (1940). *Pygmalion.* New York: Dodd, Mead.

Soloman, G. (1989, April). Hands-on science projects with help from online networks. *Electronic Learning,* pp. 22-23.

Sternberg, R. J. (1984). How can we teach intelligence? *Educational Leadership, 42*(1), 38-48.

Strahan, D. B. (1987). Guided thinking strategies for the middle-grades content areas. *Dissemination Services on the Middle Grades, 8*(9), 1-4.

Strother, D. B. (1989). Developing thinking skills through questioning. *Phi Delta Kappa, 71*(4), 324-327.

Sylwester, R. (1995). *A celebration of neurons: An educator's guide to the human brain.* Alexandria, VA: Association for Supervision and Curriculum Development.

Tobin, K. (1987). The role of wait time in higher cognitive level learning. *Review of Educational Research, 57*(1), 69-95.

Tomlinson, C. (1995). *How to differentiate instruction in mixed-ability classrooms.* Alexandria, VA: Association for Supervision and Curriculum Development.

Van Hoose, J., & Strahan, D. (1989). *Young adolescent development and school practices: Promoting harmony.* Columbus, OH: National Middle School Association.

Vonnegut, K., Jr. (1968). Harrison Bergeron. In *Welcome to the monkey house: A collection of short stories* (pp. 7-13). New York: Delacorte.

Welty, E. (1984). *One writer's beginnings.* Cambridge, MA: Harvard University Press.

Wiggins, G. (1989). A time test: Toward a more authentic and equitable assessment. *Phi Beta Kappan,* 703-713.

Wiggins, G. (1993). Assessment: Authenticity, context, and validity. *Phi Delta Kappan, 75*(3), 200-214.

Wilen, W. W., & Clegg, A. A., Jr. (1986). Effective questions and questioning: A research review. *Theory and Research in Social Education, 14*(2), 153-161.

Willis, S. (1996). On the cutting edge of assessment: Testing what students can do with knowledge. *Education Update, 38*(4), 1, 4-7.

Index

Action committees, 21
Active learning, adolescent
    thinking and, 137
Adolescence, early, xv
    cognitive changes in, 10
Adolescent learners, early:
    analysis of political ideology in,
        42
    appreciation of mathematical
        logic in, 42
    brain of, 33-35, 46
    cognitive development and,
        42-44
    cognitive growth of, 35
    determining personal identity,
        116
    developmental nature of, 9-12
    hypothetical
        reasoning/deduction in, 42
    insight into values/attitudes in,
        42
    interpretation of
        symbols/concepts in, 42

malleability of, 22
multiple concerns of, 116
needs of, 10
projecting thought into future in,
    42
propositional thinking in, 42
understanding musical notation,
    42
understanding poetic metaphor
    in, 42
Adolescent learning, early:
    as development process, 2
    as interactive process, 2
    as progressive process, 2
    thematic planning and, 114-117
Alper, L., 64
Anxiety, motivation reduction and,
    13
Armstrong, T., 41
Assessment:
    authentic, 5, 80, 95, 107
    benchmarks, 82, 84, 86, 87
    continuous, 81, 86

end point standards, 84, 87
meaningful, 81, 82, 84, 87, 91,
    105-107, 136, 137
See also Assessment, alternative;
    Developmental assessment;
    Performance assessment
Assessment, alternative, 107
    advantages of, 88
    as difficult to develop, 88
    as meaningful assessment,
        88
    as time-consuming to
        administer, 88
    See also Assessment
Atwell, N., 124
Authentic problems, 64

Barell, J., 14, 31
Beamon, G. W., 49, 55, 71, 77, 79,
    96, 97, 98
Beane, J. A., 114
Beyer, B. K., 11, 20, 22, 23
Bradbury, R., 23
Bradsher, M., 128
"Brain-drain" dilemma, 37
Brain plasticity, 8
Brandt, R. S., 19
Brophy, J., 19
Brophy, J. E., 59, 69
Bruner, J., 7

Caine, G., 8, 33, 34, 35, 36
Caine, R., 8, 33, 34, 35, 36
Carnegie Council on Adolescent
    Development, 10, 11
Carroll, L., 5
Challenge:
    as motivational, 23-24, 137
    brain and, 35
    to draw inferences from content,
        111
    to examine assumptions from
        content, 111
    to make connections from
        content, 111

to see relationships from
    content, 111
Civic action projects:
    as active instructional technique,
        14
Clark, B., 7, 8
Classroom climate:
    classroom interaction patterns
        and, 19
    classroom interactions and, 19
Classroom Climate and
    Questioning Strategies model,
    96-99
Classroom environments, safe, 18
    as challenging, 7, 12
    as interactive, 7, 8, 13
    as involving, 12
    as supportive, 7, 12
    "brain-based, 8
    characteristics of, 137
    creating, 139
    example of middle-level, 29-30
    for young adolescent thinking
        development, 7
    See also Safe for Thinking
        program
Clegg, A. A., Jr., 60
Cognitive development, learning
    experiences and, 113
Cognitive instruction, 5, 12-13, 15
Cognitive processing strategies, 71
    follow-up questions, 70, 78
    miscellaneous, 70
    postresponse wait time, 69, 78
    wait time, 68-69, 71
Cognitive research:
    and young adolescent learners,
        7-9
Collaborative grouping, 26
Collaborative learning:
    adolescents' curiosity and, 27
    communication and, 27
    design of, 27
    rigor and, 26-29
Collaborative learning groups, 26,
    145
    flexible, 31

heterogeneous structuring of, 27
structured by interest, 27
structured by like-ability, 27, 29
structuring, 27
Communication skills, importance
of, 15
Costa, A. L., 24
Creative dramatics:
as active instructional technique,
14
Critical thinking, 22
practice, 68
teaching young adolescents, 12
Curricular themes:
developmental needs and, 114
real-world connections and,
112-114
relevant, 114
Curriculum, essential elements of,
109
Curriculum development, 6

Dahl, R., 25
Debate, 21, 91
as active instructional technique,
14
Developmental assessment:
in process, 94-95
writing portfolios, 94-95
Developmentally appropriate, 5
Dewey, J., 7, 18, 22
Dillon, J. T., 50, 69
Discovery experiments, 21
Downshifting, brain, 8, 34

Elder, L., 85
Eliot, T. S., 134
Elkind, D., 51
Ennis, R. H., 22, 50, 82
Extended learning opportunities,
136

Fear of failure, motivation
reduction and, 13

Fendel, D., 64
Flexible learning approach, 15
Franquet, S., 84
Fraser, S., 64

Gall, M., 54
Gallagher, J. J., 91
Gallagher, S. A., 91
Gardner, H., 9, 28, 33, 39, 47, 80, 81,
82, 95, 116, 117, 118, 128
Glenn, H. S., 38
Good, T. L., 19, 69
Grading students, 6
Greenberg, R., 141
Group collaboration, 136
Group discussion, 21
Grouping students, 6
Group problem solving, 86-87, 106

Hagan, L., 128
Haglund, E., 9
Hart, L., 7, 8, 21, 24, 33, 34, 35, 54
Hidden curriculum, 18
Homer, 60
Howard, J., 114, 118
Hyerle, D., 128

Inquiry-based instruction, 77
teacher-student interaction
during, 77
Inquiry-based seminars:
as active instructional technique,
14
guidelines, 71-72
Instructional techniques, 6
examples of active, 14
Integrative curriculum, 5
Integrative learning experiences, 36
Interactive learning experiences, 36
Introspection, importance of, 15

Jackson, S., 98
Jackson, S. C., 23, 73, 83, 96

Jacobs, R., 142
Johnson, D. W., 56
Jones, B. F., 12, 13

Kaplan, S., 113, 117
Keyes, D., 43
Kozol, J., 79

Lane Education Service District,
    122
Lazear, D., 9, 40, 81, 91
Learning, young adolescents', 35-37
    ultimate purpose of, 132
Learning experiences, 36
Learning opportunities, 23
Lee, H., 23, 29
Little, J., 48
Logic, teaching young adolescents,
    12
Lowry, L., 16, 21, 43, 52, 108, 128

Maker, J., 40, 116
Marchioni, G., 122
Marzano, R. J., 19, 132
McBride, R., 68
Merrill, J., 39
Metacognition, 26, 76, 78
    emphasis of MI on, 41
Metacognitive skills, 51, 67, 78, 86
    assessment of, 89
    developing, 95
Middle school philosophy, 6
Multiple intelligences, 5, 118
    bodily-kinesthetic, 39, 41, 116
    interpersonal, 39, 41, 116
    intrapersonal, 39, 41, 116
    logical-mathematical, 39, 40, 116
    musical-rhythmic, 39, 41, 116
    verbal-linguistic, 39, 40, 116
    visual-spatial, 39, 40, 116
    See also Multiple intelligences
        (MI) theory, Gardner's
Multiple intelligences (MI) theory,
    Gardner's, 9, 33, 39-42, 47, 116

implications of for thinking
    instruction, 40
introspection and, 41
metacognition and, 41
reflection and, 41
See also Multiple intelligences
Multiple learning experiences, 116,
    117

Nelson, J., 38
Nielson, A., 40, 116
Norm-referenced testing:
    movement away from, 136
    versus criterion-referenced
        measures, 87-88
    versus thinking development
        assessment, xii
North Carolina Education
    Standards and Accountability
    Commission, 90
Novak, J. M., 19
Nummela, R., 36

Paul, R., 22, 50, 82, 83, 85
Paulsen, G., 21, 114
Performance, 91
    as active instructional technique,
        14
Performance assessment, 87-91
    evaluation and, 91-94
Performance-based learning, 107
Performance products, 89, 117-121
    choice and, 117-118
    evaluative criteria and, 89-90
    portfolios, 90
    student learning and, 117
Pickering, D. J., 19
Portfolio assessment approach, 95,
    107. See also Process folio
Presentation:
    as active instructional technique,
        14
Problem solving, 91
    as active instructional technique,
        14

teaching young adolescents, 12
Process assessment, xii
Process folio, 95, 107
Process questioning, 83
Program structures, 35, 36
Project Zero, Harvard University,
39
Prosters, 35
Purkey, W. W., 19

Questioning, teacher, 49-51. *See also*
Socratic questioning
Questioning-response techniques,
52-53
Questions, cognitive level of, 77
analyzing new knowledge, 55
evaluating new knowledge, 55
focusing new knowledge, 55
setting up knowledge base, 55
See also Safe question
classification model
Questions, safe:
constructing, 54-59
Question sequencing, 59-68, 71,
75-77

Raphael, J., 141
Rating oral responses, 100-103
Reading responses:
as active instructional technique,
14
Reasoning, teaching young
adolescents, 12
Reflexive thinking, 51
Reilly, D. H., 35, 40
Relaxed alertness, 35
Resek, ?., 64
Responsive learning experiences,
36
Rogers, J., 40, 116
Role play, 21
as active instructional technique,
14
Rosengren, T. M., 36
Rowe, M. B., 68

Safe for Thinking program, x, xi,
xvii, 116
acceptance of students' ideas in,
14
active learning community in, 14
adolescents' developmental
needs and, 14
applications of, xvii
as risk free, 14
assumption underlying, 2
challenge as key to, 24
characteristics of, xvii
cognitive theory and, xvii
collaborative grouping in, 26
cooperative learning activities
in, 14
expectations for students, 1
expectations for teachers, 1-2
goal of meaningful instruction
in, 139
independent projects in, 14
purpose of, xi-xii
respect for individual students
in, 14
setting, 14
teacher's role in, xi
See also Classroom
environments, safe
Safe question classification model:
A-level questions, 56
elaboration, 75, 78
E-level questions, 56
extension, 75, 76
F-level questions, 56
language arts and, 75-77
mathematics and, 64-66
physical education and, 66-67
probing, 76, 77
purpose of, 55
redirection, 75
sample A-level questions, 56-57,
58, 61, 62, 63, 65, 66, 67, 75, 76
sample E-level questions, 57,
58-59, 62, 63, 64, 65, 66, 67, 76,
77
sample F-level questions, 57, 60,
61, 62, 63, 65, 67, 76, 77

sample S-level questions, 56,
    57-58, 61, 62, 63, 64, 65, 66-67,
    75, 76
science and, 62-64
S-level questions, 55-56
social studies and, 60-62
substantiation, 75, 77, 78
textual support, 75, 76
See also Questions, cognitive
    level of; Question sequencing
Safe questioning structure, 25
Sattin, A., 84
Scales, P. C., 22, 132
Schooling, criticisms of, ix
Schurr, S. L., 10, 11, 13, 27, 42, 49,
    132
Self-directed learning, 136
Seuss, Dr., 146
Shaw, G. B., 17
Simulations, 21, 91, 106
    as active instructional technique,
    14
Socrates, 49
Socratic questioning, 50
Solomon, G., 128
Sternberg, R. J., 7
Storytelling, 21
Strahan, D., 11, 19, 51
Strahan, D. B., 13, 19, 22
Strother, D. B., 51, 60
Structured collaborative learning:
    as active instructional technique,
    14
Student accountability:
    for learning, 104-105
Student learning outcomes,
    criticisms of, ix
Sylwester, R., 8, 33

Teacher recrimination, motivation
    reduction and, 13
Teachers of young adolescents:
    cognitive growth and, 35
    interpersonal skills of, 19
    modeling thinking attitudes, 23
    problems faced by, 135

purpose of, 26
self-evaluation guide for, 15-16
structuring classroom
    experiences, 11
Teaching, interactive nature of, 19
Teaching skills, strategic
    decision-making, 6
Technology, 145
    adolescent learning and, 130,
    132-133
    as motivation for learning,
    127-130, 142
    authentic learning opportunities
    and, 128
    cognitive competence and, 130
    collaborative use of, 128, 133
    educational, 129
    high-level thinking
    opportunities and, 128
Test performance, student:
    teachers and, 38
Thematic approach in teaching
    content, advantages of, 116-
    117
Thematic units:
    as active instructional technique,
    14
Thinking:
    challenging, 51
    classroom environment and,
    20-22
    complexity of, 7
    nurturing, 51
    strengthening, 51
    See also Thinking, effective;
    Thinking, evaluative-level
Thinking, effective:
    attitude and, 22
Thinking, evaluative-level, 112
Thinking behaviors, 24
Thinking climate, creating, 9
Thinking-compatible learning
    environment, 21-22
Thinking-learning connection,
    37-39
    cognitive processing strategies
    and, 68-71

cognitive sequencing of
questions and, 68
Thinking levels:
range of in adolescents, 22
Thinking-oriented instruction, 20
primary goal of, 20
Thinking processes, students', xii
linking content and, 109-112
See also Process assessment
Thinking progress, students', 110
assessment of, xii
Thinking-responsive classroom,
example of middle-level, 44-46
Thinking skills, students':
assessing development of, xii
improving, ix
See also Safe for Thinking program
Thinking skills movement, 24
Tobin, K., 68, 69
Tomlinson, C., 109, 117

Van Hoose, J., 11, 19, 51
Vonnegut, K., Jr., 52, 60

Welty, E., 32
Wiggins, G., 9, 80, 81, 88, 89, 91, 95
Wilen, W. W., 60
Willis, S., 87, 88, 90
Writers, young adolescent:
needs of, 124-125
Writing process:
as cognitive development tool,
125
improvement as expectation of,
125-126
Writing workshops, 91, 106
as active instructional technique,
14, 126
strategies, 126-127
structured, 125

CORWIN
PRESS

The Corwin Press logo—a raven striding across an open book—represents the happy union of courage and learning. We are a professional-level publisher of books and journals for K–12 educators, and we are committed to creating and providing resources that embody these qualities. Corwin's motto is "Success for All Learners."

Lightning Source UK Ltd.
Milton Keynes UK
UKHW030330130619
344355UK00008B/212/P